Sankofa

Learning
From
Hindsight

Sankofa

Learning
From
Hindsight

By
Mensimah Shabazz

OHEMAA

First published in 2006 by OHEMAA,
Sankofa Enterprises, LLC
Copyright © 2005 Mensimah Shabazz

Library of Congress Cataloging-in-Publication Data

Shabazz, Mensimah
Sankofa:
Learning from Hindsight
ISBN 0-9786193-0-7
1. Inspiration. 2. Women Studies 3. Spirituality/
Metaphysics 4. Cross-Cultural.

Distributed by
Sankofa Enterprises, LLC
77 Crown Ridge, Newington, CT 06111

First Edition
1 3 5 7 9 10 8 6 4 2

Book design by Patricia Rasch www.patriciarasch.com
Cover art and design by Kisha McWilliams
Printed in the United States of America

For Minty

My special gratitude goes to some very special friends who did not flinch when the chips were down:
Carol Larco Murzyn
Yvonne McGregor
Horace McCaulley
S. Kimble Greene
Nancy Horowitz
Diane Litchfield
Dorothy Martin-Neville

For guidance:
Sophie and Peniel

For love and stability:
My mother, my sister Essumanba and my late brother Essuman
My Family
My Friends
My Teachers
My Sisters
The Staff & Faculty of the Institute of Transpersonal Psychology for bringing meaning and enrichment to my life experiences especially
Dr. Irene Lazarus, my mentor;
Dr. Michael Hutton, Dr. Nancy Rowe, Dr. Henry Poon, Dr. Kartikeya Patel, & Rosalie Cook

Special Acknowledgements:
Nikki Costello
Pamela Edwards
S. Kimble Greene
Anne Murphy

PREFACE

In Ghana's Akan tradition, storytelling is an almost daily occurrence. Anecdotes and fables educate, teach, advise and shape communal behavior. Each story is meant to touch the listener's heart. It is believed that the community suffers if an important story is not shared. Important stories focus on heroic or notorious themes common to the public lives of men. The private stories common to the domestic lives of women are seldom, if ever, repeated. To do so would be immodest and attract unsuitable attention.

As a young Ghanaian woman, I accepted that only men's stories were told. Experience taught me that it was usually in my best interest to keep my story to myself. So I lived in silence, sharing neither my pain nor my joy, until my story was lost, even to me.

As I grew older, I taught myself to focus on the future. My desire to see the outside world got me out of Ghana at a young age. I spent time in Europe and South America. Eventually I settled in the northeast United States and my future looked bright. I was adjusting well to American culture. My career was blossoming, and I shared a beautiful home with my daughter. My friends and family admired and supported me. Then, on a winter shopping trip, I took what I thought was a harmless slip on a patch of ice. As it turned out, I had seriously injured my spine.

As my spine collapsed, so did my perfect life. Excruciating physical and emotional pain left me totally disabled. I couldn't walk, and I couldn't work, no matter how hard I pushed myself. I had lost the independence I valued so much. Money was getting short and I was in danger of losing the possessions I relied on for my self-worth. When I looked inward for spiritual strength I'd known as a child, I found that I had replaced it with self-reliance. In anguish, anger and confusion, I cried out to Spirit. *Sankofa* was my answer.

Easily thought of as the wellspring of Akan storytelling, *Sankofa* is thoroughly expressed in the Akan language as *se wo were fi na wosan kofa a yenkyi*. Literally translated, *Sankofa* means "it is not taboo to go back and fetch what you forgot." The symbol of *Sankofa* is a bird flying forward while it looks back to where it's been. The message was clear: If I hoped to heal, I would have to go back and fetch the story I had spent my whole life forgetting.

As I surrendered to the spirit of *Sankofa*, I was continually humbled by its depth and wisdom. A spiritual path revealed itself to me and propelled me toward universal consciousness. Teachers and friends appeared seemingly out of nowhere, blessing me with support, strength and inspiration. Simple yet awe-inspiring answers and guidance came to me through my dreams.

Through *Sankofa* I have discovered that my story is heroic and illustrious in the private way that many women's stories are. It may attract unwanted attention. But more importantly, it will also touch hearts. If I fail to share it, my community surely suffers.

The Magnificat in My Own Image

I was born in the month of November
As the elders describe, that is the month
where if one goes through
is able to live and tell their story.
I was blessed with a rich imagery of depth and permanence
when my birth coincided with a fixed water element
as my astrological sign.
I was named Amma for a girl born on Saturday
and was honored with the name Esi Mensimah,
my grandmother's name.
And my soul rejoiced.
Culture and tradition appeared in every fiber of my being
with drums speaking to my heart.
I learned that I could whisper through the wind to talk with the
Goddess and she appreciated the proverbs,
songs and rituals that honored her.
This indigenous religion reinforced my belief
that human progress brought
peace and harmony in my community.
And my soul rejoiced.
With a powerful physique
I was endowed with great love, sensitivity, mystery and wisdom.
As the eagle was introduced to accompany my journeys,
I learned to love with fierce abandon.
My heart opened and burned with passion for love and justice
And my soul rejoices for what is yet to come.

Mensimah Shabazz, 2002

CHAPTER I

The Beginning

I was born in November, 1955, in *Oguaa* Cape Coast, Ghana, the West African nation where rocky lagoons, forest bush, and grasslands ring with the sound of *Hi-life*, the richly diverse, traditional music of the land; where drums announce celebrations, births, deaths, marriages, and the church harvests; where pouring libation and dancing is tradition; where ritual, myth and superstition are commonplace and Spirit is honored in life and in death.

As the Akan tradition teaches, I was born with total awareness of myself. Waving my tiny fists over my head, I yelped with all my might to draw some attention from the women who had just helped my mother with my birth. They looked at me suspiciously, saying that such strong lungs would need to be controlled. In Ghana, adults do not like strong or showy personalities, even in newborns, because they indicate a lack of humility. Without hesitation or qualms, the midwives made the traditional announcement of my birth. "Vin has a girl!" they shouted to those just outside the door.

My custom also teaches that I was born with a full awareness of whom I was meant to be. But after the announcement of my birth, I fell into a deep sleep, forgetting everything but how to survive, cry, eat and develop relationships with nature and the people around me. Since then, I have been awakening, remembering the wisdom that was mine with my first breath.

As tradition demands, Ghanaian children know the day of their birth. It is believed that a child assumes its spirit name on that day. I was named after my paternal grandmother so I assumed my spirit name and inherited hers as well. The middle and last name of a child bears the father's family and tribal lineage. My first name, Esi means a girl born on Sunday. Men-si-mah is a name from the Fanti tribe of my father in the Central region of Ghana. Later I was baptized and given an English name, which had no connection to who I was as a Fanti. By the time I reached high school I refused to use it and answered only to my grandmother's name, which gave me a direct link to my ancestors.

A few years after I was born, my father became seriously ill, and as is common in those circumstances, I went to live with my maternal grandparents. Grandpa Sardis was a very tall, thin, light-skinned man. We called him *Papa Nii*. He wore clothes imported from England, which I saw no other person in town wear. He was well-liked and well-known. He owned the main shopping store in our town, *New Tafo,* and the next town *Old Tafo,* with the regional center in a town called *Koforidua*, as well as several cocoa farms where employees worked for a percentage of the produce and earnings. He also owned a few other buildings in all of these towns. These buildings were rented to several families. In one compound, he had about eight families, some of whom paid nothing. There were no evictions. My grandparents were gentle, kind and loving people as their traditions taught.

Apart from the flourishing business and community presence, he played a quiet, yet powerful role in shaping the politics of the town and several neighboring towns. One interesting story we were told growing up was about the role he played during the national elections to replace the colonialist government. The British threatened not to pay workers in our town if they went to vote instead of coming to work, which frightened most of the workers out of exercising their rights. *Papa Nii* paid the salaries of over one hundred employees to enable them to vote. There were no strings and it proved to be a worthwhile investment. With this stature, it was not surprising that we were known in town, but never by our names. We were Sardis' grandchildren. Whenever introductions were made, the details of who we were started with his name, his daughter or son's name, and then our name. They would say "This is Sardis' daughter, *Adjeikai's* youngest child" and the elders knew exactly how to make the link.

My grandmother's name was Susuannah. [Suswana] We called her *Mammi*. She nursed the ill with medicinal plants picked from her yard. She cooked delicious meals, and we had people eating in our home any time of the day. She could look at the sky and tell the exact time of the day. She was pure and honored Spirit with every act.

In our community, eloquent men performed most of the ritual pouring of libation. Women, in their silence, gave food to the gods and ancestors in more frequent, but less conspicuous ways. I remember how *Mammi* would thank Spirit for the blessing of water by pouring some on the ground before taking a sip.

Because there was a clear delineation between the social responsibilities of men and women, I grew up observing how women spent time with each other. On a typical Sunday after church, the women's fellowship would hire a brass band, and dressed in their traditional attire with white wraps around their heads as priestesses, they would dance through the main streets of town. It was one of the few times that women were willing to express emotion openly and joyfully. They smiled, waved and danced to the rhythms of the band. It was a union of women celebrating each other, a circle of empowerment.

Because of her social and financial position, *Mammi* had several women, and a few girls who had just passed puberty, living with or working for her. The adults were usually ready for marriage. The young women and adults would spend the day with her and she would teach them to be good homemakers. Her financial status was not solely due to my grandpa. She was, in her own right, a successful businesswoman. She made pastries – *sweet bad, atsomo, too gbee* – and these were distributed to the local markets in neighboring towns. *Mammi* also had the largest cooking pots I had ever seen! I saw her use these pots often. During funeral ceremonies, where families would have several out-of-town guests, she would cook enough meals for them so they would not have to worry about preparing food. She never charged for these meals, nor did she wait to be asked.

We had a big compound, and, to my young eyes, it was a paradise. The compound formed a semi-circle with the main house on the left ending with the guesthouse to the right. Within the semi-circle were concrete walkways connecting all of the buildings. To close the circle, there was a big outbuilding of about four to five thousand square feet where my grandfather stored some of the cocoa bags ready for export. Playing "Hide-and-Seek" in this hall was the best when it was possible to climb onto a pile of cocoa bags a few feet off the floor.

Papa Nii's office was in front of this shed. The aluminum barrier that enclosed the compound was softened with pink bougainvilleas and hibiscus. The front garden of the main house was a profusion of tropical plants and flowers. To the left corner of the wall, there were sugar cane, pawpaw, avocado, guava and cocoa trees. The backyard had plantain, banana and palm trees, as well as vegetables. There were fish in a pond and a brook running through the yard to the back of the fence where wild cocoyams grew. Between the front gate, the guest building and the main house was a manicured lawn, cut and trimmed by the garden boy.

Just to the right of the gate was an orange tree and right in front of the guest building was a mango tree. All of the trees bore fruits yearly, and it was fun watching them ripen right before my eyes. The main house was a bungalow. It stood on strong concrete pillars and was painted green and white. It included the main bedrooms, living room, dining room and pantry, all with hardwood floors, polished until they reflected a person's shadow. The living room extended from one end of the house to the other and was brilliantly and luxuriously furnished. The main house was also reserved for special entertainment. The breeze flowed gently through each room, as though grandpa's kind and loving spirit controlled it.

The second building had a living room and a bedroom. The third building had four bedrooms and two living rooms attached. One side was rented out to family friends and the other was our guesthouse.

We had many guests passing through our home. Some were family visiting for various lengths of time, and some were total strangers passing through town. None of the strangers was ever turned away. There was no screening process to determine whether a guest might be unstable or dishonest. They were all given fresh towels, and baths were prepared for them. The beds in the guesthouse, like any other bed in the household, were always made with starched white sheets washed and ironed by the *washman* named *Kpalisu*. He was very tall and lanky, and I sometimes wondered where he found the strength to wash anything. But he did his work well.

My grandparents' generosity and kindness taught me how important it is to give generously and share with others, regardless of class or social differences. They never asked for a guest's gratitude. Although it is extremely unusual for a Ghanaian guest to leave without thanking my grandparents or eating breakfast with the family, some left at dawn without as so much as a goodbye. This unusual behavior did not deter *Papa Nii* from opening the door to the next visitor.

The three smaller buildings in the compound contained the maid's quarters and three kitchens, toilets and bathrooms. There was a spare room for the fowl to sleep in at night. Very late in the evening, the watchman strolled in with his mat and flashlight to stand guard and deter intruders from entering. He seemed almost too tired to stay awake, but he convinced himself that there wasn't a chance he could fall asleep chewing cola, which contained a lot of caffeine.

As a very young child, I was happy and secure. Every morning *Mammi* woke up at dawn, and I awoke with her. She would put me on her back, wrap a cloth around me and tie it tight in front of her. She carried me that way for hours while she and her girls did the morning chores. The gentle rhythms and warmth of her body were so comforting that I would fall right back asleep.

After *Mammi* finished her morning routine, I would be bathed and dressed by the maid. Then we would travel on a local truck to *Old Tafo* to spend most of the day with my grandparents' firstborn son and his family. Climbing into one of the trucks required skill. The maid would balance one foot in a hole about three feet off the ground while hoisting the other foot several feet onto the bench. In all it was about a four-foot climb, and everyone who could, mastered the trick. I was glad that I was young enough to be carried on board.

After several years of these trips to the next town, I started school. When classes ended around noon, I would be picked up by one of my grandmother's girls and brought to her at one of my grandfather's shops. Sometimes she was at the UAC (United African Company) store and other times at the cocoa shed where several of my grandfather's bags of cocoa would be prepared for final shipping to the city. The cocoa brought in a lot of money. The UAC store closed off the compound to the front where my uncle and aunt lived. This house was also very well designed. The yard, however, was separated from the main house by a concrete wall. The plants, fruits and gardens were to the right of the house and had well-manicured paths to walk through. It was an ideal place for adults to have private conversations, or just a peaceful walk. I would run through the gardens as if it were my first and last time because it brought me such joy. The same design was used in my grandparents' home in their hometown of *Teshie* and our vacation trips there to enjoy the summer festivals were a real treat.

As a school-aged girl, my daily routine started bright and early. At this age, I was expected to be more independent, but my grandparents were always nearby. I was out of bed by six in the morning. I was required to wash my face and mouth, and clean my teeth with *saawe* before speaking to anyone. After that, I was expected to complete my chores. I usually swept the compound, made a fire in the clay stove and put fresh water in a twenty-gallon cast iron pot. We were blessed to have running water.

When my chores were done, I took my bath. Because I was still under the age of seven, my baths were supervised by older women and taken outside in the open. The women taught me the art of bathing, and I was allowed some playfulness. I would splash the water, feeling its freshness on my body. I was also taught to layer my skin thoroughly with a fine coat of shea butter, taking my time to bring out my skin's suppleness.

These simple lessons of bathing and massaging my body were supervised before breakfast and supper. During those times, I was taught the appropriate lessons for a young girl blossoming into womanhood, and I began learning to honor my body and Spirit.

Just before I turned five, my mother came to live with us in my grandparents' home. She brought my older sister and brother, whom I did not remember at all. When I asked about my father, I was told he was traveling. I was hushed into silence by my aunt *Araba*. We nicknamed her *"Boja Master"* meaning fire-cracker, because she was quick to discipline and was less tolerant of inquisitive questions from children. I liked her because I knew where I stood at all times. She did not seem afraid of anything. At times, I saw men being drilled into submission by her no-nonsense attitude. While my mother, and especially *Mammi*, would be uneasy about some type of punishments, Aunt *Araba* did not flinch.

Behind her stiff exterior, she was very caring. She was tall, with a very dark skin-tone and extremely beautiful. To her, toughness of mind was the most important attribute anyone could have. She insisted on taking hot cooking pots off the coal stove without using a dishcloth to prove her point. It was a contentious idea to ask the rest of us to imitate that. When she walked through the gates we all readjusted our behaviors by making sure we did everything well. She was the next best cook to grandma. Aunt *Araba* exuded confidence in everything she did and whenever she visited, *Mammi* would graciously allow her to take over and supervise the preparation of meals for the household. Her *palava* sauce or *kontomire* (stewed spinach with dried salted fish) with plantains made everyone's mouth water.

As soon as my mother arrived, my life began to change. On one hand, I maintained the same relationship with my grandparents and was closest to them. On the other, my mother became the authority figure and set new rules for the children, one of which was silence. Upper-class Ghanaian women and children are expected to be quiet, so my mother's attitude was not uncommon for women of her status. Still, I was a curious child and talked endlessly. Several times my mother ordered me not to speak while she was in the house. I felt frustrated because I had so many questions and ideas floating through my head, which I needed to resolve.

In contrast, my grandmother encouraged me to express my curiosity and sense of humor. Together, we worked out secret communications with our eyes, or the exchange of a few words. For instance, even though *Mammi* was forbidden to have tobacco, she liked to occasionally hold a bit in her cheek for a few minutes. To avoid getting caught removing it from its hiding place, she would signal its location to me with her eyes, and I would get it for her. Of course, it troubled my mother that *Mammi* seemed to always have a supply of the forbidden substance. I could not resist my grandmother's sweet smile however, and we both got great pleasure out of our little games. One of the happiest moments in my childhood was seeing *Mammi* laugh so hard at something she would hold her left hand over the side of her stomach as if it hurt.

I could, in some situations and without effort, behave as gently and lady-like as my mother wanted. At those times, I got the nickname *fofoi* meaning flower. My brother and I played together often, and he unselfishly taught me many games that the boys played, including soccer and hiking in the bush. Much to my mother's dismay, I often bore the marks of the unconventional escapades of a young, free-spirited girl. The bandages around my ankles looked like socks in photographs from that time.

In spite of my scrapes and wounds, and my mother's admonishments, I never hesitated to go on the next adventure. I was driven to search, understand, or unravel some of the reasons behind the rules and traditions that did not make sense to me.

I found other ways to go outside the compound, but I did so with my grandpa on his morning walks around town. He had long strides, and I sometimes hopped next to him to try and match them. He chuckled at my efforts. The other exciting adult relationship I had was with my grandpa's youngest son, *Wofa,* meaning "uncle". He was silly, and spent most of his visits playing with us. Not many adults did that. The men sometimes idled in conversation over beer or palm wine, and the women were too busy with chores. Playing was the last thing on their minds. *Wofa's* presence was refreshing, and being the youngest of my mother's siblings, allowed him to take a carefree approach to living. He traveled a lot even though I was not so sure what his occupation was. After saying a quick "hello" to *Mammi* and *Papa Nii*, he would naturally gravitate towards his nieces and nephews. He would dance, make faces and tell dramatic stories of his trips away from home, which made us giggle with excitement. His presence often softened the discipline and seriousness of other grown-ups in the compound.

My mother also had 'allies' in her war against my rebellious nature. Ghosts play an important role in the Ghanaian culture, and ghost stories are common. As a child, I learned that ghosts were often ancestors who would be displeased if I misbehaved when I thought no one was watching.

One day, after picking berries from the fields of the Cocoa Research Institute, my brother *Papa Bibio*, cousin *Sowah*, a few of their friends and I were walking home, which was on the other side of the train tracks. As we came close to the junction of the railroad station, I saw a pale couple walking a few feet ahead of us. They looked like the albinos I had seen in town. They walked very fast with their necks and backs straight. Their heels barely touched the ground. No one I knew walked like that.

Confused, I tugged at my brother's shirt, but he ignored me. He was in a deep conversation with his buddies and had no time for his little sister who followed him everywhere. I decided to take matters into my own hands. I sprinted a few yards ahead, hoping my companions would come after me, but I heard them laughing as I got farther away.

Frightened, I began to run towards home, my legs spreading to their full length. The sounds of the drums in the distance matched the pounding of my heart. I dashed across the tracks, forgetting to look for a train. In what seemed like a record-setting pace, I ran through the gates to our private compound. Everyone noticed the anxiety in my voice and panicked, thinking someone was hurt.

As I gasped for breath, my chest heaved and my ribs hurt. Because I was so skinny, it had become a family past time to take turns counting my ribs, each person coming up with a different count than the one before. But this time no one played that game. They just looked puzzled as I tried to explain that I had just seen ghosts! I was only seven years old, and probably too young to have seen a ghost before, yet I seemed so certain that no one could think of any other way to explain my experience.

I bent over with my hands on my knees to catch my breath. *Mammi* sat in front of the main kitchen behind a table near the coal pots while mother, walked towards me almost in a panic and asked in her native language of *Ga*: "*Maame Esi, mini éba?*" "What has happened?"

"What is the matter?"

I could not respond. I was breathing so heavily, it hindered my speech. I just pointed to the gate.

"Is someone hurt?" Mother asked quickly and I responded by shaking my head from side to side.

"What is it?" I could sense the urgency in her voice.

"Ghosts"! I muttered softly, and then continued. "I saw ghosts!", I said, this time with more conviction and emphasis. Just before I was barraged with more questions, my brother and his gang strolled in, laughing at my expense. They explained my behavior and after a sigh of relief from everyone around,

I could hear mother suck her teeth, a common adult reaction to frustration. "Tsssssssssssssssm!"

Perhaps these ghosts were there to torment me because I hadn't finished my chores before following my brother and his friends into the woods. Maybe, I had teased too often, or challenged my brother and cousin to play soccer or table tennis one too many times. I knew I was wrong to climb the mango tree in the yard. I had the unlady-like scars to show for it. In addition, I had tried climbing the coconut tree before scraping the skin on my thighs, which had caused me to give up. What if these ghosts were punishing me for being such a disappointment to my mother whose expectations of having a lady for a daughter were shattered by my tomboy behavior?

While my grandmother and others looked amused, my mother looked annoyed. She obviously thought I was whimpering over nothing, but no one could calm me or change my mind. They explained that my ghosts were *obroni*, meaning white people, who lived at the Institute.

Now, in addition to feeling confused, I was ashamed of my ignorance. Until that moment, I had never thought of anyone, including myself, as a color. But it was true that the *obroni* couple had light-colored hair brushed down the back of their necks and nearly transparent colored eyes. They walked differently, too. This was a land where walking was deliberate and slow. The wiggling gait of women who carried their children on their backs, and the premeditated steps of the men who planted their feet firmly on the red soil – those were the gaits I knew.

I had lots of questions, but could not pull them together to make any sense, so I simply dismissed the whole experience from my mind. I was young, and it was time to play again, this time with the girls. '*Tu-e tu-e ma-mu-na tu-e tu-e*', we sang and clapped.

After a quick bath and a supper of cornmeal, hot pepper salsa and fried fish at sunset, it was time for storytelling. When that night's ghost stories were told, I snuggled tighter into the bed cloth wrapped around my body. As far as I was concerned, I'd had enough of ghosts for one day and skip-walked quickly to bed so no more could find me.

After the *obroni* confusion, I was still curious about why everyone was afraid of ghosts. I would wander and meander through back alleys and short cuts on the way home from school, often coming across someone laid in state. I once snuck behind the rented row of chairs to observe a funeral. The professional weepers swayed from left to right, backwards and forwards, crying so loud yet without a tear, while other mourners sat and drank beer under tents to cool down from the strong rays of the sun. Nothing seemed to be happening in these places to indicate that ghosts were harmful, and I left with more questions and disappointment.

If I had been caught by any adult or had talked about that escapade, I would have had my ear tugged until it ached, or been lectured for days. Children were not allowed to respond when adults talked and lectures were meant to discourage further mischief or quell notions of a repeat performance. I was lectured a few times. The punishment got worse if any adult reported an observation of my behavior, which was considered out-of-line. These observations were subjective but I was still punished by having more chores and that mellowed my knack for mischief. But all these seemingly tough punishments made me more curious. I just worked harder not to get caught.

My cousin, *Ashami,* and I were the youngest children in the house, so we had the privilege of bringing clean towels and other toiletries to guests. We often wondered whether the strangers were really human. We always looked at each other right before knocking on the door and ran very fast out of the room with our arms in the air to escape the unknown possibilities of having met a ghost. We sometimes convinced ourselves that we had seen one if we noticed an abnormality in a guest who grinned too much, or looked too serious.

My grandpa died when I was in class four. His absence left a vacuum and emptiness in my life, but I could still feel his presence in the compound, in the gentle breeze that blew through the main house. I often thought his spirit protected me from ghosts. Our sadness deepened as my oldest uncle *Adjei'apa* died soon after grandpa. Before things returned to normal, if they ever could, my favorite uncle, *Wofa,* also died in an accident on a ferry at *Aflao.* In the blink of an eye, all of the significant adult men in my life were all gone, except for my uncles *Klu* and *Kwame,* who lived in the city.

With my grandma aging and sad, my mother took over the day-to-day affairs of running our home. The cushion of comfort, gentleness, laughter and joy I had known with my grandparents was gone. In my mother's style, everything was done with a fiery swiftness and precision, which left no room for errors. There was a tyranny of perfectionism; very little room was left to chance or humor.

From culture to culture, the trials of being a single parent vary little, and parents everywhere make mistakes out of love for their children. Widowed young in the summer of 1958 and before my third birthday, my mother had three small children to raise by herself. She made enormous sacrifices and met many challenges. Already a strong-minded woman, my mother's hardships only strengthened her resolve not to give in to her fears or doubts. Everyone in my grandmother's house learned to adjust to the new environment. Laughing about errors, or any lack of seriousness, was unacceptable. In spite of my mother's no-nonsense attitude, I was still stubborn and rebellious.

Having snacks around three in the afternoon was always fun. We had a lot to choose from, but one of my favorites was sweet Portuguese bread and butter, or Ovaltine rolled in our palms till it was sticky and chewy. I was not supposed to eat Ovaltine that way, but that was the way I liked it. Once, we had a young maid who was new in the house. As I rolled my chewy chocolate crunch, I realized she had never tasted anything like that before, so I gave her some.

My grandmother preferred water biscuits and once when she had asked for her snack, there were fewer biscuits in the box than there should have been. Immediately, my mother started asking all the children who might have taken *Mammi's* biscuits. We all denied eating them. To our taste they were dry, plain and tasteless, but for some reason the maid told my mother that I had given her some. I hated water biscuits and explained to my mother that I had given her ovaltine. She didn't listen, and I was given an ultimatum: to confess or go without dinner. I refused to confess to something I hadn't done.

For about four hours I sat quietly, hoping that my mother would weaken. I was desperately hungry.

When my grandmother advised me to just confess so I could have dinner, I almost gave in. Instead, I explained to *Mammi* that I did not give the girl water biscuits and could not say I did. I went back to sit on the stairs, still waiting for my mother to find another form of punishment rather than have me starve to death. At 10 p.m., I still had not had dinner. My grandmother urged my mother to give me some food, and while she hesitated, *Mammi* went ahead to warm a plate for me. I was so angry by then that I could not eat, but I would not give in. That night I learned that I was willing to sacrifice for honesty. I also earned credibility with the family, and my truthfulness was never questioned again.

When my mother took over the house after my grandfather's death, I was sent to a new school. I left the A.M.E. Zion Primary School and joined class six at the Methodist Primary School where mother taught. I walked about a mile home every afternoon at noon to help *Mammi* with lunch, then walked back to school for the afternoon session. Nothing escaped my mother, and while I would enjoy the same jokes and silly games all kids of my age played, I always knew I was under her watchful eye. But I competed very well in class and was a very good student, so we had no problems there.

It was in this new school that I first became aware of my family's social status in comparison to the other pupils'. Every Friday the teachers picked the student with the neatest uniform. I had many uniforms and could have changed twice a day if I'd wanted to. But that was not the situation for the majority of the students, some of whom would wash their uniforms mid-week and then show up the next morning half dried. Some students had only one uniform, which began to show wear and tear towards the summer. Even though I did not sense any animosity towards me, I was embarrassed to be singled out every Friday as the student with the neatest uniform. I felt ashamed and wished I could escape the spotlight.

By the end of the school year, I was ready to transfer to the town's middle school, away from my mother's watchful gaze. But there was yet another surprise in store for me. All the arrangements had been made for me to go to boarding school like my sister and older cousins. I knew nothing of boarding schools, except that I would be living there during most of the term. I was ten years old, too young to be leaving home. I felt lost.

CHAPTER 2

Growing Pains

It was late August 1966, before my eleventh birthday, when my aunt "*Boja Master*" accompanied me on my trip to boarding school. I had a metal trunk and a wooden box with my initials inscribed on the front. My clothes and some toiletries were in my metal trunk. The wooden box, which we called *chop box* contained provisions such as canned milk, sugar, *garri*, hot pepper sauce made with dried shrimps, ginger and hot chilis. The extra food would serve as a supplement for lunch or dinner in case either meal did not look appetizing or taste good. After we arrived in the new town, *Kumase*, we took a cab to the school. She left me within minutes of our arrival. Her only advice was to "stay well".

My new home was called *Mmofraturo*, meaning "The

Children's Garden". There were nine houses with three large bedrooms in each house. Eight girls slept in the main bedrooms and four girls in the middle room. I was in house number seven, and while I thought seven was my lucky number, I quickly realized that in this case it would not bring much luck.

The girls in each house participated daily in different activities including sports and gardening. Going to church was a "must", unless you were admitted to the sick bay located in the headmistress's bungalow. Almost every Sunday, except on our monthly visit to the Methodist Church in the center of town, we marched like little toy soldiers to the church at Wesley College next door. We sang "When the Saints Go Marching In", or "We Are the Famous Girls," when we wanted to show off to town folks, who knew of the prestige of the school.

My first year at *Mmofraturo* was a nightmare. It was my introduction to understanding the meaning of overwhelming emotional pain, worry and sadness. Although I had experienced some unhappiness at home, those times were always balanced with pleasure and play with other children. At *Mmofraturo,* the living conditions were almost unbearable after the beauty of my grandparents' compound. The bare concrete floors with no tint of color, and the half sized doors with low ceilings seemed built for adolescent girls with growth deficiencies.

My house prefect, the leader of the house hazed me constantly. I remember the way she looked the first time I saw her. She was tall and very mature. Although some Ghanaian children start school late, I had never seen anyone that old in middle school before. My astonishment must have shown on my face, because from that day she singled me out for torment. She enjoyed assigning the toughest jobs to me: scrubbing floors, weeding bushes and leveling the gravel outside the house. Sometimes as soon as I finished leveling the gravel, the students would walk on it leaving new sets of footprints and I would be called to redo the work.

I wasn't used to such heavy manual labor. My body ached and my hands blistered. I was also assigned dining hall duties, which included serving the stew for supper and washing dishes. One day, after picking up a dark brown meat stew from the kitchen to the dining room, I left the stew on the bench instead of the table and went looking for my ladle. Someone walked by the bench and knocked the stew over. I was so scared. Fortunately, all the other girls serving stew put some of theirs in my bowl, enough for my housemates. But my house prefect told everyone not to eat. Instead, she had my chop box opened, which was full of *garri*, *shito*, sardines, canned corned beef. My house prefect, her friends and some of my housemates, while laughing emptied and trashed everything else they did not need. The only security I had disappeared into thin air. I was stunned to see the level of cruelty exhibited. Even though I was not the only student experiencing these hardships, I was in such a deep hole, I was unable to observe how some of my classmates coped with the new experience.

Before long, my stomach turned just at the sight of the prefect and her closest friends. They preyed on the fears of young girls with ferocity and viciousness that I did not know could exist in any human heart. One evening, they dragged me into the bed of one of the seniors. She had a gap in her teeth and her eyes bulged out of their sockets. She was scary to look at during the day and much more so at night. When I got there, I was told to lie down, but I stood, wondering what was going to happen to me next. I was shoved into bed. The rest of the women left, laughing their way out of the hall.

I shivered, even though it was a warm night. I had brought my sleeping sheet with me as I was ordered to do and was grateful for it because it was new, clean and quite comforting. As I lay there, I had no idea what was coming, but I knew it was not good. These women did not do good things. When I closed my eyes, I could feel my bedmate's hands sliding down my spine. She whispered softly into my ear not to be afraid. But that made me more scared. It was like being tricked by the devil all day, and then she comes during the night to tell you to trust her.

With my sheet tightly wrapped around me, I cried silently until I drifted off to sleep. I did not move all night and woke up stiff and achy. This was a total stranger I had absolutely no liking for. She was mean [during the day], ganging up with other women of her age group to torture the younger girls. They teased us and ran their fingers down our faces so hard they stung.

Even at night, there was no peace. The bathroom and toilets on campus were located behind the middle houses. To get there meant walking at least twenty yards from my house. There was a tall nim tree in front of the bathhouse that reached into the sky and hovered over all the buildings around it. Legend had it that owls, witches and ghosts from the cemetery across the road fed and roamed there each night. A slight ruffle of leaves sent many girls scuttling for cover. Like many of the girls, we were fearful of stepping out at night but we were still not sure what it was that we ran from, except from our own, old and concocted superstitions.

I wondered how a Christian institution could be riddled with such fear of ghosts and witches. But imported and imposed ideologies were out of sync with our traditional beliefs. Even though colonization introduced us to different ways of worshiping, we all grew up traditionally first, and our beliefs were deeply rooted.

Long before I came to this school, my sixth sense was quite pronounced and I had the ability to see 'things' and hear sounds. Most of my premonitions were about things I did not know much about which made it easy for my family to believe me.

I noticed in pictures taken during those youthful years that I had a bright spot on my forehead, the size of a half-dollar coin, and was nicknamed 'headlamp'. I was "led" by the "lamp". It felt like I had a miner's lamp in the middle of my forehead and I related to its presence more than any other part of my body. I felt the vibration of it and was very aware of its prominence. The nickname "headlamp" seemed appropriate because it described accurately what was physically visible. Of the many photographs we took as children, I always saw this lit spot and it was undeniably different. It was my intuition that led me to explore – looking for possibilities.

On many occasions, I made comments about people visiting the compound randomly which seemed to have an impact on the grown ups more so than on me. I was so young and yet

I gave vivid descriptions of 'things' or people I saw without any prior knowledge of who they could be but *Mammi* and my mother knew and understood. In fact, neither questioned the things I said, ever. Others reacted to me with stunned silence.

One story that I vividly remember was about a neighbor whose husband was ill. He was taken to the hospital and was admitted. He lived with his second wife and there were rumors that the first wife had poisoned him because she was jealous. Since my family knew the second wife, both *Mammi* and mother did everything to support her during this difficult time. When the man was discharged from the hospital and brought home, I caught a quick glimpse of him. I felt a heavy tug in my stomach and told my mother about it.

There was a suggestion made by the man's family to follow up the hospital treatment with a visit to the witchdoctor. Witchdoctors use herbs and other tricks of the trade to treat their patients and while this may have been an unusual venue for my mother, she was determined to support her friend. After her return home, she described the experience, which seemed to have affected her greatly. Even though children are not privy to adult conversations, she seemed to be directing her doubts about the process to me, almost asking for "confirmation" that everything would work out well. My concern at that time was more on the heavy feeling in my stomach. "He is not going to make it", I told mother innocently. She looked at me intently and asked, "Are you sure?" I nodded affirmatively. The man died within a couple of weeks after that "prediction" and I felt scared. Even though there were more predictions and descriptions of things I saw, I felt more out of place. The lack of belonging I felt based on my unorthodox behavior as a girl and my gaffes about seeing things made it difficult for me, even though I was never discouraged from doing so. I began to experience fear whenever what I had to say was negative. There was a burden that was associated with those predictions and I may have made a subconscious decision to stop talking. I did less and less of it with time. I barely said anything at all by middle school and I would not have dared to say anything at *Mmofraturo* based on the pressure and energy there.

I wrote many letters to my mother, begging her to remove me from *Mmofraturo*, but my pleas fell on deaf ears. At the beginning, most of my letters home would have a misspelled word, or bad phrasing, of no consequence; yet, my mother would correct my oversight in red ink and mail the letter back to me. Her only comment about my troubles was that the "hardships" were good for me because they would make me a stronger person.

I realized, at some level, that in spite of all the mistreatment at the school, I was privileged to be in such a prestigious school. It was one of the best girls' middle schools in Ghana, and sending me there was very important to my mother. I believed that she was ignorant of what really went on, that I was being molested. All she wanted was to provide a good foundation for my future, and I was not going to disappoint her.

Over time I developed ways of coping with the constant harassment. At night, I switched beds so that I would not be dragged out again. During the day, I hid my feelings behind a tough exterior until I felt almost nothing at all. Before long I was able to forget any unpleasant experiences almost as soon as they were over. Because I did most things well, no one noticed that I had become very quiet and withdrawn.

Apart from the girls in my dorm, I did not form any strong alliances with anyone, which was quite unusual for me. I had always been a very outgoing girl who spoke her mind easily. By my second year in the school, I had learned a lot both in class and by being away from home.

The long, lonely trips between school and home hardly mattered anymore. I began to look forward to my escape from *Mmofraturo*. All I had to do was pass my entrance exam for high school, which I was confident I would do easily. But just about a week before the exam, I broke out with chicken pox. The blisters started in my scalp and spread heavily around the trunk of my body. I was quickly isolated from the rest of the students and remanded to the sick bay. I was not allowed any visitors, and even though the sick bay was a relief from the hard routine of the dorm, I was so bored out of my mind that I shaved my eyebrows.

Still determined to pass my exam, I continued to study as well as I could. But on the day of the exam, I was told I could not go because I could still infect others. I asked questions about what would make the difference and found out that the blisters had to change into scabs. After the discussion, I went to the bathroom, scrubbed my body raw, got dressed and left the sick bay. I did not care what the consequences were at the time.

When I arrived at the hall where the exam was being held, most of the students had started their first paper. The proctor was very kind. He gave me a table in the corner of the room, away from the rest of the students. I managed to get through the exam, but I was exhausted and my whole body ached. I snuck back to my bed and slept soundly the rest of the afternoon.

The test results were sent directly to the students' homes. As parents started to arrive at the school to tell their daughters which high schools had accepted them, I waited for my mother to come. Although I was confident that I had passed the exam, I waited nervously for my mother to come tell me where I would be going next. One morning, after what seemed like an eternity, I saw someone who looked like my mother walk into the administration building. I was not absolutely sure it was her, so I decided to go on with my business and not raise my hopes. As I settled in to my class, the headmistress sent for me. I knocked on the door, and wanted to peak through a window to get a hint of why I had been summoned, but all the window shades had been drawn tight.

The headmistress finally opened the door and gestured for me to enter. My mother was sitting there. I curtsied and put my arms behind my back, a British custom that was common in upper-class schools and designed to instill discipline in young girls.

This was my mother's first visit to *Mmofraturo* since I'd been sent there two years earlier. She did not know where I slept, who my friends were, or how I survived each day. Now she sat only a few feet away from me, absolutely still, not allowed to give the traditional greetings or show any emotion. If she had, the headmistress would have intervened. Part of her job was to train young girls in the stiff European style brought to Ghana by the British.

Educated Ghanaian women of my mother's and headmistress's generation struggled to find a balance between their traditional culture and the influence of the British. They did not bathe or carry their daughters as their mothers had. They emulated the European habits and style that could help their husbands advance in their careers [as men were more likely to copy the attitudes than women] within the much-entrenched colonial system. Knowing this, I was not surprised by the lack of opportunity to embrace my mother and it hurt. I still desired the warmth and tenderness my grandmother openly shared.

As I had taught myself to do, I quickly set that emotion aside. The headmistress coldly informed me that I had passed my exam to high school, and they needed to take my measurements for my new school uniform. My heart leaped with joy. At that moment nothing else mattered. My daring move to get out of the sick bay had worked, and I was on my way out of *Mmofraturo*. I refer to my departure from this school as the 'great escape', because I did not have any recollection whether I said "goodbye" nor to whom. I packed my trunks dutifully; making sure that nothing would compel another visit. I walked to the waiting taxi and I did not look back.

For a long time I never mentioned to anyone that I went to "The Children's Garden". All that mattered was that I had walked out alive and "sane". I was so proud of my achievement that, even though nicknames are not common in Ghanaian culture, I began calling myself "The Great." I might have had Alexander the Great in mind, but I'm not sure. My mother was astounded, but to this day she greets me with "Hello, The Great!"

I was nervously excited that summer. I had to begin preparation for yet another boarding school and had no idea what I might encounter at this one. I was optimistic that even though it might be tough the first year, I had some knowledge of how things worked. I knew that I could charm a senior into becoming my friend and protector. Left on my own, I would either fight my way out of difficult situations or simply forget them as I had at *Mmofraturo*. By this time I could summon almost total amnesia on cue.

CHAPTER 3
Changing Landscape

The surprises that had begun at *Mmofraturo* did not end there. There was a new twist. It was 1968 in independent Ghana when I traveled south to my high school and found that it had nearly an all-white faculty. There was only one black teacher on campus. The British teachers had acquired all the power; the American Peace Corps volunteers were as interested in learning as teaching, and there was only one affable Canadian teacher. Although there were a few teachers who went out of their way to get to know us individually, most respected a strict British protocol at all times. Speaking vernacular was strictly forbidden. My classmates were a fun, close-knit group. We stuck together, finding humor in every little mishap, and I began to enjoy being at school more than being at home.

Because my mother was a teacher and principal, the people in the community who chose to follow the British-styled educational system expected her to not only discipline her children but to also make sure all her students behaved appropriately both in and out of school. Parents from the whole town turned to her for advice on how to enroll their children in schools that would teach them proper British etiquette. And of course she expected my sister, my brother and I to set a good example.

With this level of responsibility and pressure, she had become so serious all the time it was impossible to breathe when she was around. If we looked too happy, she would ask if we were ill or find some work for us to do.

I remember being home during the Easter holidays of my first year in high school. One sunny afternoon, I felt a throbbing pain in my lower abdomen. After a little while, I saw blood in my underwear. I knew what it was because I had seen most of the girls in school go through this. What I did not know was that it could be painful. The pain was so intense, that I soaked a towel in ice water and put in on my stomach. But I still had to rest for a few minutes between chores. When my mother called me to do something, I walked out and did whatever it was without showing that I was in pain. I managed to get money from my grandmother to buy sanitary towels because I was afraid to tell my mother that I'd started to menstruate. But when she wanted an explanation for why I'd asked my grandmother for money, I had to tell her.

Custom required that a girl who comes of age must eat certain foods for the day. I was served *oto* – mashed white yams in palm oil mixed with onions, peppers, spices; and a boiled egg, which was delicious. I tried to hide and was embarrassed when every visitor to the house was told that I had become a woman.

Soon after, on one of my errands in town, I noticed a young girl wearing the traditional ceremonial bead necklace that indicated she too had just become a woman. Her plum breasts peeked out from the edge of the beads. Her supple skin shone under the brightness of the sun, showcasing her silky buttery body massaged with shea butter. Her waist was adorned with heavier beads of warm colors. Between her legs hung the ceremonial stole covering the pubic area and the middle of the buttocks, which were smooth and gracefully curved.

I knew that she had enjoyed an evening of celebration with family and friends. As was the custom, she would have danced with gestures that expressed her gratitude to the earth, her ancestors and the gods that she had become a woman. That afternoon, her mother walked with her, letting it be known that she was now willing to accept suitors for her daughter.

As I watched the two of them, I compared my day of hiding from visitors to this beautiful display of tradition. I wondered if I would ever feel the pride and dignity that shone from the young woman. She was truly Ghanaian. I was neither Ghanaian nor British. I just felt lost in my simple, less colorful but well-tailored British clothing. In a twist of irony, she probably would have preferred my European look to the almost-naked garb. And this twist and clash of culture was found in many aspects of Ghanaian life; in school, how we dressed and behaved; and it became more complicated with social status.

I had become a young woman who knew what was morally acceptable in my culture. I had the advantage of a good education and a stable home life. I respected the authority of my elders and was discreet in my actions. I had spent years away from home, but I was always with women and still very naïve about men. Although I knew about sex, I did not know about rape.

I was in my third year in high school and fifteen years old. I was traveling to school and I had decided to make the long trip in one leg instead of the usual plan of staying overnight at my auntie's house. I left home at dawn, after saying goodbye to my brother, grandmother and mother. My mother knew our town's bus owner who was also traveling that day and entrusted me into his care. When I arrived in the city, I had a few hours to wait between buses. I was tired and it must have shown, because the concerned-looking bus owner approached and told me he had a place I could rest and that he'd wake me up when it was time to get on the bus to school.

Because I had seen so many guests in my grandparent's house, it did not seem odd to me that this man would invite me to follow him into a house where everyone seemed to know him. He even had a room ready for me to lie down. The furnishings were plain compared to what I was used to at home, but I was grateful for the chance to get a couple of hours' sleep.

The room was warm, and I slowly started to drift off to sleep. I heard him come into the room with a glass and water and leave. When he came in again, I thought he was just checking whether I had settled in. But as I turned into a more comfortable position, I saw he was naked from his waist down and was leaning over me on the bed. Shocked and bewildered, I had very little time to react before he raped me.

As he got up to leave, I sobbed quietly. I hurt so bad, and I was so raw that it felt as if my skin had been peeled off. I tried to smooth my crumpled dress. I had never worn a crumpled, stained dress in my life, but I did not have anything to change into. I was confused. I had not seen a naked man before and had no idea they could do such things to young girls who had been entrusted to their care. I also knew that girls who had sex at a young age were bad, period.

I walked to the bus in a trance, with sadness and a broken spirit. The bus conductor pointed to the departing bus with my luggage already loaded onto the rack. I had learned at *Mmofraturo* to keep my pain inside, but that afternoon I could not hide my sullen mood. I sat near the window in a daze. The new driver knew where I was getting off, and by late afternoon the bus pulled in front of the administrative building at school.

Aching and ashamed, I walked towards one of my friends. As we helped each other settle in, she could not help but ask whether I was all right. I almost told her, but afraid that she might insist on getting help, I assured her that I was all right. For days I was very quiet, and even though people expressed concern, I could not talk about what had happened. Instead, I tucked the memory away in what I thought of as a pocket in my heart and forgot it for many years.

After a few weeks, I was back to acting like my old self. But inside I felt abandoned because I was unable to talk to my mother and there was no other adult to whom I could turn. My feelings were confusing. Although I had accepted that my mother would not demonstrate warmth and affection openly every now and then I hoped that she would attend parent teacher conferences at my boarding school which were often fun affairs. In fact, a few times she traveled past my school, she stopped briefly to drop off a parcel at the front office and left without seeing me. The idea of being 'spoiled' by that attention prevailed.

I had grown up learning not to cry or show any signs of my pain because it would be perceived as weakness. So I simply forgot my disappointment and had no other expectations. I was satisfied that she had provided everything I needed both in school and at home and may never discuss anything emotional. I had become what I thought was a strong person, able to surmount any obstacle. I accepted that in spite of the nice clothes, good home, prestigious schools and friends, I felt alone. My only option was to take care of myself.

I had always been a good student, but about half way through the school year, I began to lose interest in my classes. I found that it was easier to keep my spirits up if I spent most of my time playing. If I was still for too long, I felt like I had stepped in quick sand and was sinking slowly. For the first time in a very long while, I thought of my father. Would he have protected me at the bus station? Would he have listened to me? I would never know, but I'd found a way to comfort myself: "If only he'd been there. If only..."

At the end of the term, school was about to close for the summer, and for the first time I did not want to go home. I was willing to live on campus even if it meant I would be there alone. After my futile attempt to persuade a few close teachers to let me stay, I wrote to my mother in an act of desperation and told her how I felt. I wrote that living at home was more difficult than living at school. I hoped that she would be concerned enough by my letter to relax the discipline around the house for a while and let me enjoy a little fun. I was afraid I would break after everything I had endured.

I did not get a reply to my letter, and I knew something was terribly wrong. When I got to my aunt's house I learned that my mother was so upset with my letter she asked that I not come home for a while. I felt bewildered by my mother's decision. While I was blamed for being disrespectful, no one ever asked what could have prompted me to write the letter. It had nothing to do with her, really. I was crying out for help.

Family intervention in resolving issues is traditional and routine in Ghana. After several family elders consulted with my mother to ask for her forgiveness on my behalf, I was told I could go home. As soon as I walked through the gate and saw my mother's face, I knew that no matter how much I loved my home, my life there was going to be worse than it had ever been. I wanted to leave immediately, but there was no place to go.

Now my mother was even more distant than she had been before and her discipline more on point. I wished I could restore our relationship to what it had been before, but because I couldn't talk about what had happened at the bus station or any other time, I had no idea how to begin. I had already gone beyond the boundaries of respect by hinting at my real feelings in my letter. I was miserable. Within days I had become so despondent that even the usual pranks with my brother were of no interest to me.

By now, the only people that lived on the compound were *Mammi*, Mom, my brother and I. My sister had left, as had all the other cousins. *Mammi* and I had become closer as my brother spent time with grown up boys. I had no interest in being a part of the group, nor would it have looked proper. *Mammi* would find an activity for me to do and sometimes share the history of some of her possessions; why she purchased certain *aggrey* beads and which ones were her favorite. My mother was busy with school, church and other social activities.

Surprisingly, someone had noticed my lack of interest in a lot of things at school and mentioned it to the headmistress who wrote a letter to my mother, advising her to accompany me to school in the fall. I picked up the mail that day and I could not let my mother see the note. After several days of pondering and discussions with my brother, we came to the conclusion that burning the note was the only way to avoid my mother's unpredictable reaction. I still could not talk about what had happened. When school reopened, I left alone. During a visit to class, my headmistress seemed surprised no one came with me, but I was able to avoid talking about my mother's absence.

That semester I was so miserable that I contemplated suicide rather than suffer even one more emotional assault. I had never felt so desolate. But while I pondered the ways I could do it, I realized that if I followed through I would be known as a weakling, and that was one thing I could not let anyone say about me. I had survived *Mmofraturo* and all the other things I did not care to think about. I had nicknamed myself "The Great," and great people did not kill themselves! So I focused on the fun things around me.

Mr. Haviland, my math teacher, and Miss Vaughan, my English, shorthand and typing teacher were in love. They blushed each time they walked past each other in the hallway, which got all the students hopelessly excited. Imagine being in a school where being formal, prim and proper was the norm, with two lovebirds caught in an unavoidable exhibition of emotion. We giggled and teased them a little to increase their embarrassment. Most days, we had English class right after math so they passed each other at the classroom door. During the few moments they spent in the doorway, they tried to disguise their feelings, but it was hopeless. All the girls went beyond silly. We clapped and hummed English love songs, scribbled love notes on the board and signed their names to them. They were young so they did not mind our teasing them, even in vernacular.

Mr. Sinclair had a beard and decided to shave it all off at the beginning of the school term. No one recognized him when he walked in class, and that opened a discussion about the disappearance of a beard halfway through the period, while he sat with a smirk on his face. He enjoyed the attention! That was the first time we had an *obroni* shave off a beard, and he looked so much younger that we were totally confused. Most of us thought that we had another math teacher with the same name! But that idea did not hold water, so we went back and forth, and because we were so engrossed in the discussion, he made no attempt to teach the class or correct the situation. Sometimes we directed our questions to him. He refused to answer, sitting there with a huge grin on his face. That finally gave him away. Of course, by the time we finished our discussion, the period was over, which pleased us very much.

My least favorite teacher taught biology. She had us hunt for live toads to be dissected in class, whilst the jarred toads bemoaned our discomfort. For preppy girls like us, it was a crime to touch animals. I thought the request to hunt for toads was odd even for me because I had spent a lot of time outdoors, and in nature, and touching animals, as a girl was not condoned. We cried during class wondering what possessed her. Some girls were so scared they let go of their toads and we all jumped up our tables and screamed. This got her so mad, she had us weeding bushes with machetes for a week. We had blisters and bruises to show for it.

By the time I finished high school, I had developed a strategy for responding to anything that could cause me pain. Before anyone had an opportunity to assault me either verbally or physically, I lashed out. I became impatient and less likely to feel the same level of empathy I had before. I avoided intimacy in many relationships and cut people off my list for the slightest infringement. Before long, I developed a reputation for being ruthless, temperamental, and overly sensitive.

Love was a word that was totally missing from my vocabulary at that time. When asked once by a friend whether I believed that through all the strictness and harshness, I knew I was loved, I honestly did not know what to say. The idea of being loved had never occurred to me, and I didn't understand the question. Looking back, I know that I loved my grandparents, my mother, siblings and cousins. As was our custom, however, no one ever talked about love. In fact, up to that time, I could only recollect one direct compliment, and that was from my former headmistress. In a job reference, she described me as being "a lively, active student in class and socially, pleasant and good-natured, with a very open, friendly personality." I was stunned and so deeply touched when I read what she'd written. At least there was one person who saw me for whom I really was, in spite of my tough exterior. The headmistress' comments were only complimentary and did not necessarily demonstrate love, but in a society where everyone was silent about the subject, and especially as it related to children, I made that association.

After high school I was accepted into Wesley College, which was right next to *Mmofraturo*. It was mother's preference. Of course, I refused to go. Proximity to a place that had caused me so much pain was not an option I was willing to consider. I had no intention of re-experiencing my feelings from that time. Also, most of the country's best teachers were trained at Wesley and many of them supported the system against which I was rebelling.

Because my mother did not know what happened to me in *Mmofraturo*, she was perplexed by my refusal to go. For several weeks, she worked hard to convince me to see the wisdom in that choice, and for several weeks I dug in my heels. Again, family intervened to try to talk some sense into me, but the more they did, the more I resisted. Finally, after promising to return in September and attend a different college, I was allowed to move to Accra, about seventy miles from home, for a summer job at the Research Library on African Affairs.

Before working at the library, the only books I had read about Africa expressed Western views. Now, I would rush through my work and read books on Pan Africanism or the African National Congress. The subject of Pan Africanism or the African National Congress had neither come up in my studies, nor in conversation. Yet, by the time I graduated from high school, I knew U.S. geography, European trading practices and, of course, everything about the Roman Empire. I had been taught about the beginnings of Christianity, the Methodist church and John Wesley. I had learned about important monuments that were named after English missionaries like David Livingstone. I had memorized Macbeth, Julius Caesar, and other verses and poems by Shakespeare, Bronte and other Western authors. But I could not write my own language, beyond the few texts I'd learned in middle school.

I had been taught that Ghana was irrelevant, that it was totally dependent on Western nations to survive. Yet, as I sat in the library and read, I learned that Ghana's per capita income was higher in the 1960s and 1970s than that of some European nations. I learned that our own history, or religious practices, and good people who were as benevolent as John Wesley had been erased from my history. My generation had spent a lot of time mulling over news on the BBC and Voice of America. Even though the exposure had its good points, it encouraged a tainted view of our world.

As I discovered my continent's history, and the basis of

our spiritual beliefs, I felt that I could now express legitimate arguments about the ills of colonization. Right then, I committed to creating new systems that were more supportive and respectful of African culture and traditions. I would make sure that my children would know the true history of our people. I would honor its beauty and its flaws, rather than the narrow Western view of a country in despair.

What was even more significant to me was the pride in recognizing that my connection to my ancestors was deeply rooted. I had felt it strongly, beginning with my decision to use my grandmother's name in high school. I also recognized, politically, that as we took pride in our leaders from *Nkrumah* of Ghana to *Kenyatta* of Kenya, *Kaunda* of Zambia, *Ben Bella* of Algeria, *Modibo Keita* of Mali, *Alhaji Sir Abubakar Tafewa Balewa* of Nigeria and others, it was not about the competence in how well they maintained the British system, but it had more to do with nationalism, patriotism and solidarity of our culture. It was noted in the traditions of language, attitudes and spirituality. Unlike my mother's generation, we had a choice to balance our traditions and culture with the dignity and splendor of our ancestors.

In September I was ready to go back to school. I had been accepted to The Institute of Professional Studies (IPS), also located in Accra. Since it was a private school, the director tightly controlled everything, including the academic criteria, which followed the British system. I had been in British-style boarding schools for several years by this time and expected IPS to be just more of the same. I was not disappointed. College was uneventful. I loved literature and I did well in my management courses. However, I was tired of dorm life and spent most of my time studying or being with my boyfriend.

Afriyie was the new addition to my life. We had met in high school when we were both on our schools' debating teams, and my school was hosting a round of debates. We had never spent any time together until he began working in Accra while I attended IPS. He was an intelligent, confident young man, and we had the same interests – sports, books, music, dancing and social issues. When we disagreed on an issue, we could debate it without rancor. He often teased me about how much more Europeanized I was than he.

We were both very stylish, and we looked very well together. He was tall, about five feet ten, with very dark beautiful skin and strong. He walked with a smooth and elegant sway of his shoulders. I was five feet eight with a light brown skin tone. I had always said I could not date a shorter man, and most Ghanaian men are short, so I felt lucky to have attracted *Afriyie*.

This was the first attempt at courtship for both of us, and it was awkward in the beginning. There were no Akan rules against premarital sex, and a man is held responsible for a pregnancy no matter what the marital circumstances. Though the church opposed premarital sex, I did not feel any moral conflict. So as we grew fonder of each other, it was inevitable that we would consider making love. Even though I wanted to make love and express what I felt for *Afriyie*, I had to get past the psychological barriers caused by the rape. We talked about it for a long time and kissed a lot. During some of those times, I almost revisited the rape, so it was a long time before I agreed to be intimate.

Afriyie seemed pleased with himself after our first sexual encounter. He blushed through his dark skin, talking about what a night it was, while I wondered what all the gloating was about. I had hated every minute of it. I could not explain why and was not sure what it was that I was supposed to feel. I honestly expressed my disappointment, and he was puzzled by my indifference. I will never forget that conversation.

We talked often about our first night and my feelings. *Afriyie* tried everything to make me comfortable. He brought me gifts, was very affectionate and showed that he was proud to have me as his girlfriend. We made love only if I agreed, and I trusted and believed that he really cared. But, for a long time, I was still ashamed of doing anything. My shame was partly because of my lack of interest. I wanted to be close to him and thought that I should enjoy our intimacy. And as we spent a lot of time together, I made progress. We made love from time to time, and because we shared several interests, our relationship became more interesting and quite nice. We were inseparable for four years.

My relationship with *Afriyie* changed after I graduated. I had a very good job working for the managing director of a major corporation. This corporation was playing a vital role in the economic and social structure of Ghana at the time. As the director's executive assistant, I handled administrative functions for his office, including scheduling meetings with General *Kutu Acheampong*, a former President, ministers of state and other corporate executives. My job provided me with a driver and a one-bedroom flat. After so many years in boarding school, it felt wonderful to be in my own home. I furnished it in good taste. I had learned decorating skills from my grandmother and mother. The cushions in the living room were warm, earthy colors, my bedroom furniture was custom designed and the bed sheets were crisp white. My mother saw that I was at last living like a lady and was very proud of me.

Afriyie moved in with me and seemed to enjoy the benefits that came along with my job. He became worried, however, about the possibility that I would meet someone else at work. He began questioning me constantly. Most of the time, I ignored him, but his tantrums began affecting my career. He started leaving his workplace during the course of the day, ostensibly to bring me my lunch. I was flattered because few Ghanaian men are that romantic. As it turned out, he was really there to watch how I behaved around these "powerful" men. He complained that I smiled too much and was too nice! Everything – the way I dressed, my makeup, visits home – became "too" something. Thank heaven I had my own office and didn't have to explain *Afriyie's* tantrums to my boss.

Afriyie enjoyed my cooking and would sometimes bring his friends over for a meal, which I did not mind. One day he brought home his younger brother who was visiting from another city. He stayed with us, and as he settled in, *Afriyie* started showing off the flat as if he were the master of it. After he and his brother ate, *Afriyie* left the dishes in the sink and then stormed into the bedroom, complaining that there hadn't been enough meat in the stew for both of them. He told me to cook more food next time, enough for at least four, and buy drinks for the house so he could entertain. On and on and on his list of demands went.

He talked at the top of his voice so his brother in the next room could hear him. But this tantrum was a big mistake. He had not yet contributed a penny to the household, nor had he cleaned the flat since he moved in. He was freeloading, and for him to have the audacity to complain was more than I would tolerate. I still lived by the decision I'd made in high school to never again let anyone bully me or ignore my feelings in a relationship. So this one had to go.

In a soft, assured tone, I asked how much he thought it cost me per month to feed him. I did not give him a chance to reply, but without raising my voice, I laid down several other facts that he had conveniently glossed over. By the time I was done, he sat stunned, apologetic and ready to please again. But my mind was made up, and I gave him a reasonable length of time to move out. Our relationship started going downhill from that point on, and we could not save it.

While dating Afriyie, I also continued my visits home to visit my mom and *Mammi* as often as every other weekend. I enjoyed these interludes. My relationship with my mom had improved tremendously and I had a new appreciation for the strict way she handled things. I realized that I easily transitioned into many activities with confidence, both socially and academically.

My relationship with *Mammi* had deepened even more. I was the closest granddaughter and I accompanied her on her walks, feeling very protective of her. She had aged gracefully, and had maintained her sense of humor. Often, when mom would comment on her use of tobacco, she smiled with a twinkle in her eye. I had a feeling she appreciated my knack for mischief.

On one of my visits, I noticed that her health was deteriorating and needed more medical care. The family doctor visited her at home every morning and would spend a great deal of time, sometimes just chatting. The end seemed apparent to me when she started talking about seeing *Papa Nii* in her dreams. She often said she could see him standing in her room every so often. While some thought she was delusional, I believed her. I could sense the energy.

The last weekend prior to her death, I was with her. I walked into her room, and sat on her bed. She held my hand and talked about grandpa again and her late sons. In a way, I felt she was saying goodbye. I did not want to her to see me cry, but as she dozed off, with our hands still clasped, I could not hold back the tears. I walked into another room and wept. I knew that would probably be the last time I saw her alive and it was. The doctor had indicated it could be any moment. As is with tradition, there were close family and friends who came by to pay their respects. There are silent prayers as well as singing.

I received a call in the office on Wednesday that *Mammi* had died. I was devastated. She was 86. I left work immediately. My boss gave me several days off, until after the burial. I traveled back to *Tafo* to be with Mom. The pain in my chest was immeasurable and my hands just shook. As I approached the compound, the townsfolk departing whispered "this is one of the granddaughters," as they had done all our lives. Some shook my hand and others curtsied to show their respect. I walked through the compound as if I was lost. To the community, a matriarch, a "mansion" of wisdom, had passed leaving a legacy of gentleness, generosity, respect and love. To me, I had lost more than a grandmother. She had loved me unconditionally for all of my life. Every word she uttered was gentle, loving and supportive. She had shared her wisdom with a humble demeanor.

I greeted all the people in the house, one handshake at a time. Crying silently, I saw my mother first at the top of the stairs and we embraced. She said to me *"Maame Esi, Mammi eshi wo"*. *"Mammi* had left us" and she broke down and wept with me. She had been so busy attending to the guests that she hadn't had a moment to react to her emotional pain until she saw me. As she had requested prior to her death, *Mammi* was transported to Accra while funeral arrangements were being made. Her final resting place would be *Teshie*, her hometown. My mother accompanied the body, and I stayed behind to greet visitors who came by to express their sympathies. In spite of the influx of people trailing in and out of the compound, it felt empty.

During those few hours, I realized what a strong bond the three of us had shared. In closing this chapter of my life, I recognized that my first memories of my childhood were with *Mammi*, and I was overwhelmed with emotion knowing that this was the end of our physical relationship. I could not stop crying and it got worse as people continued to weep all evening. My mom arrived about nine in the evening and realized what an emotional mess I was. For the first time in years, she told me how proud she was in the way I took over the responsibility in such difficult circumstances.

My presence was also consoling for her and I was especially proud of her for the sacrifice she had made all those years in looking after *Mammi*. I found her commitment to her mother, both in personal attention and in her career, noble. She had very little help during that time.

The number of people that showed up to her funeral was impressive. After the ritual bath, the wake took place as always, on Friday evening ending at dawn. The drum beating the familiar sound of "*damirifa due*" was overwhelmingly sad. Even though I had heard the low heavy drum beats several times before, they resonated to the core of my being. I had not experienced pain so intense.

There were important rituals performed at funerals where mourners had conversations with the dead either through their tears or "mumblings". The words were incoherent to my young ears, but the elders understood every word. The procession to the church was particularly difficult. I chose to walk behind the hearse, instead of riding to the church, and I still had not found a way to stop crying. I did not want to leave the gravesite. There was such finality to the process; I just did not know how to comprehend what I was feeling.

When we arrived home, the celebration of life had begun. Meals and drinks were served. There was dancing and more drumming. As I retired to my flat and to work, I knew my life had changed forever. I would not see again *Mammi's* sweet smile, nor will I feel the unwavering support and unconditional love she showed me all my life – from the days of the "piggy ride" to my adult life. I did not show my emotions outwardly, but I cried often when I was alone.

CHAPTER 4
Making Adjustments

After *Mammi's* death, and breakup with *Afriyie,* I met the most beautiful man I had ever seen and started dating again. *Youssef* was from north of Ghana. He had a captivating smile, and was one of the few African men I knew who could wear European or traditional clothes equally well. We worked in the same corporation, and I was courted over a period of time. He was well educated and headed one of the departments. It seemed that other women had as much trouble resisting him as I did. I found out later I was just one of his many girlfriends at the time. His excuse was that, as a Muslim, he was entitled to marry four women, and since polygamy was traditional in our culture, most women accepted it.

I always felt conflicted with *Youssef,* especially about dating, marriage and the way he treated women in his relationships. I felt the tradition that allowed men to express love and interest to more than one woman was emotionally abusive. But that was what persisted in the lives of women, both historically and emotionally. I knew I did not have what it took to be married long-term in this type of relationship, as well as do all the things expected of me as a woman. Women worked hard, and they did everything, literally. If jumping through the hoops could assure one of having a sound relationship without the emotional hassles, one might feel some reward for the sacrifice, but it was never enough.

The typical *Ghanaman* would not hesitate to remind his woman of his right to live a polygamous life, or to openly feast his eyes on other women. I thought I preferred to be the lover or second wife. The lover or second wife had a better deal most times. Either way, it was a "lose-lose" relationship. When I realized that I was falling in love with a man who would always have many lovers, I was very disappointed.

To console myself, I went to an Italian movie in which the man was so in love with his lover that he was willing to die for her. I felt that his expression came from the depths of his soul, and that was what I believed all lovers should experience. I knew that I wanted that kind of passion and emotional involvement for myself. I made up my mind before walking out of the Orion Theatre that I would travel to this place where the expression of feelings, passionate social engagements and discussions were the norm.

There was much opposition to my leaving, but I was not deterred. I could not say goodbye to my mother because I did not want to see her angry or, most especially, sad. My sister had already left home with her husband, so I left my brother to do my dirty work for me. On a Friday evening, I boarded a flight for Rome.

I arrived in Rome soon after the death of Pope Paul VI in 1978. The city was electric with the excitement of burying one Pope and electing another. I was excited about participating in all the activity even though I wasn't sure exactly what it all meant. At times, I thought that I must have been out of my mind to leave the security I had known for feelings evoked based on a movie. Those kinds of thoughts frightened me, so I spent very little time on them.

I thought about what I saw in my new environment and compared it to the place I had come from, and felt almost somber at the stark differences between the two. The former proudly exhibited a society that lived and survived purely on the desire to preserve, restore and build new structures that were artistic, creative and bodacious, which also reflected the personality of people that lived there. The latter still struggled with and almost seemed lost, in her efforts to shake off the effects of colonialism, even after "independence". I had seen pictures and images of buildings in the old kingdoms of Ghana and Mali and other parts of Africa before the arrival of the Europeans and they were uniquely designed with elegance and traditional flair. All the pride and creativity that went into designing those buildings seemed to have dissipated into thin air.

I was soon settled at the home of a staff member of the Ghanaian Embassy. Within the first few days, I had visited all the places I felt drawn to even though I'd never seen them before. I saw churches, old ruins, the Appian Way, the splits and bridges across the Lungotevere to Trastevere, with my tour ending at the romantic Villa D'Éste. I spent many hours lost in comparing the sights and sounds of Rome to what I had left behind in Ghana. Rome was a place where emotion was expressed exuberantly, with hands, voice and heart. Life was sometimes chaotic, even over small matters, but it was a friendly chaos. In Ghana, expression was reserved, no matter what we felt inside.

The first church I visited was Santa Maria Maggiore. The Gothic doorway was impressive, but I had this sense of sadness as I walked through the divided nave with its fifth century mosaics. I rested in the church until I felt peaceful. As I walked out, I knew this was going to be a real adventure. My first goal was to find a job, and I had done some homework before leaving Ghana. I knew the ambassador, so I gave him a call. Although I had no real understanding of diplomatic language, my heightened interest in politics made the diplomatic mission the perfect place for me to work. I settled down and learned the protocol very quickly.

One Saturday afternoon, the meat shop in my piazza was packed and in trying to avoid the line, I decided to go to the smaller meat shop outside the square. I saw only red meat there, but I thought that would do for my meal for that weekend. I asked for a pound of the meat and went home to cook. I boiled the meat for a long time and it seemed tougher than anything I had prepared before. When I bought an English/Italian dictionary, I went to that same shop to ask for lamb. The owner, speaking only Italian said *"Qui, c'è solo cavallo."*

While I tried to search for the meaning of *cavallo*, she pointed to a picture on the wall. I saw only horses in that picture! She nodded to confirm the frown on my face. I did not eat red meat for a very long time. With the deep sense of adventure that I had, I knew that I would one day stumble on something uncharacteristic and this was it. I had eaten horsemeat and I was not amused!

I also watched American westerns dubbed to perfection. I started building a vocabulary of words that could get me around town. Pope John Paul II, with his boyish, sweet look and a glimmer in his eyes that gave away his potential to be mischievous and fun, was now in the Vatican. I took that as a sign that Catholicism was not all solemnity and droning chants that nearly put me to sleep. Here was a reason to look forward to the holidays.

It was almost Christmas and the weather was getting very cold. My coat did not keep me warm enough during the day, but I had the most trouble sleeping at night. I shivered till my teeth chattered. The layers of clothes, including mittens, hat, two woolen blankets and a comforter did not keep me warm. The standing electric heater dried my throat and skin. I missed the calabash full of shea butter at my mother's house. I was so miserable that I took my first straight shot of cognac. It didn't help.

I made arrangements with friends and my cousin in Geneva to spend the holidays together in Rome. They were guests of one of the counselors at the Ghana Embassy in Rome. On Christmas Eve, I was picked up by the counselor to join the girls at a few embassy parties. One thing that made me proud was the cohesiveness of the African diplomats. We partied together and enjoyed the rhythms of the Congo, the fast beats of Senegal, the majestic sounds and voice of the incomparable Miriam Makeba and the jazzy sounds of Hugh Masekela. The hour-long songs from Nigeria's Fela Ransom Kuti and his Africa 70 band always brought everyone onto the dance floor. His bold and humorous lyrics incited some interesting discussion about politics and social issues. Of course, one cannot enjoy a good party without the sexy, hearty Ghanaian hi-life with its traditional West African drumming.

As an African, even in the midst of a cold season in a strange land, any opportunity to interpret the rhythms and lyrics of the music with people who understood the cultural presentation could not be missed, and I was really enjoying the dancing. So I may have gotten carried away, but life was good and I let myself enjoy my new life. As I shook my hips in sultry gestures that reminded me of home, I felt for the first time what courage I had shown by leaving. I had just turned twenty-three, and in my short life I had experienced many things, both joyful and painful. Now I had become a strong woman who could stretch as tall as she wanted. I was creating the life I wanted for myself, and I knew I would succeed.

After the party on the way home, something strange happened. The counselor stopped at a busy intersection and asked me in a quiet voice to get down from the car. We were laughing and joking so without a second thought I got out, thinking that he may have spotted a police car and did not want to be stopped since there were six of us in the car, or maybe it was a joke. My friends seemed to have the same thoughts, so there were no protests. But as I stood on the street, he drove off. I watched the car disappear into the night and realized I had been abandoned. I could not believe the situation I was in.

I had left my night bag and address book in the house when we left for the party. I did not remember the address off the top of my head. I knew the name of the town and area and started hitchhiking. It was a dangerous thing to do because there were several ladies of the night lined up on the street, looking for clients. A few drivers who stopped were clearly furious that I was not looking for company. Finally, I got a lift from a young soldier going in my direction. I had been stranded for several hours now and was exhausted. This young soldier spoke French, and as we drove around eliminating houses in the area, my high school French came in very handy.

During the ride, my angel in uniform never gave me any reason to worry or be uncomfortable. When we found the house several hours later, he promised not to leave me until I got inside, which was very comforting. As I approached the house, I thought for the second time in a few hours how, even in the face of danger, I did not seem as anxious as I had been during my boarding school years. But I was angrier than I could remember being at any other time.

As I walked into the house, the girls were sitting around the table in the kitchen and seemed a little restless. I told them how disappointed I was, especially since my presence in that house was only arranged because of them. From the corner of my eye, I saw the counselor approach, and I pounced on him like a tiger.

In Ghana, the traditional way to handle a situation like

this would have been to ask another adult to try to resolve the misunderstanding. Sometimes this process worked, but other times this resulted in being told to just let things go. "*Efee noko* or *onye hwee*," they would say, "It doesn't matter." But this did matter, and I was not in Ghana. I felt proud of expressing my feelings and standing up for myself.

For a while I did try to come up with an explanation for why the counselor had left me at the roadside that night. As far as I knew, there was only one. As we danced that afternoon, there was a particular song that one danced with movements resembling a limp. Even though I started the laughing and limping, almost every one joined in. This counselor had a deformed leg, which made him hobble, and he may have concluded that our antics were directed at him. It was almost too bizarre to think that he believed we would all make fun of his condition. It made me laugh that he would rather leave me by the roadside than speak openly about how he felt. Because I expressed my feelings in confronting him, I gained the strength and freedom to move on emotionally. I also decided to make several changes to my social life.

In my job, I had the opportunity to meet a lot of people from different parts of the world. I surmised that taking advantage of that would be interesting and beneficial. I started hanging out with a whole new group of people – a few Romans and others from English speaking countries. I learned how to bowl and drink Irish coffees, which became a Friday ritual. On Saturdays we traveled to different towns to tour, taste wines and try out Italian gourmet restaurants.

At night we went dancing. On one of those Saturday nights

we were joined by a new group of friends, and as we were being introduced, I caught the eye of an Italian fellow named Bruno. He was young, with dark brown hair and big brown eyes. He wore tinted glasses, tight blue jeans and a striped light blue shirt. The front buttons of his shirt were open, revealing the hair on his chest. Black men don't usually have hairy chests, and even though I hadn't been thinking about dating, especially with a white man, I couldn't take my eyes off him. We danced most of the night. My Italian was getting better, but I soon found that I did not have to think about that. He spoke English. We were as different as night and day, but intrigued with each other.

He drove me home that night and several more nights after several dates. I thought of my "*obroni* ghosts" and my fear melted away as I realized that people are all the same. After all, don't we breathe the same air provided by the universe; have the same color blood running through our veins?

My relationship with Bruno blossomed into everything I envisioned a love relationship should be. We were partners and went to dinner two to three times a week. His mother packed picnic baskets for our weekend trips outside of Rome. I adored our weekend escapes to the valleys and the gorgeous Alban hills of Frascati. We made several trips to the pleasant Tivoli, which was purely "Romanesque". Villa D'Este stood out at night with its sixteenth-century frescoes and the soft sounds of water from the avenue of a hundred fountains. For two summers, we trudged a road out of Rome to Castel Gandolfo, located on the west shore of Lake Albano. The happiness I felt brought memories of my childhood when happiness was expressed in every fiber and muscle in my body. It reminded me of my adventures in the woods with my brother, the scary yet joyful entanglements in trees.

I enjoyed this new freedom. I grew up in an environment where holding hands in public drew stares from both young and old. Our Ghanaian sense of romance bordered around secrecy, and everything that had anything to do with sex and love were concealed. But I did not want to import that culture into my new routine. With time, I eased into the spontaneity of the moment and enjoyed my freedom.

For the first time in a very long time, I was relaxed and everything seemed to be in its rightful place. I liked my new apartment, which had such a spectacular view of Rome. I ate dinner at the homes of the residents in my apartment building. It became a contest to see who could feed me more often. If I dodged dinner, I had food sent to my home from several neighbors. I liked my new job at the Zambian Embassy and was fascinated with the manipulations and usage of language in the world of diplomacy. I had the opporunity to meet His Excellency Kenneth Kaunda, President of Zambia and one of the statesmen and engineers of freedom for Africa. I even loved the chaos in the city and everyday life. In contrast to my life at home, it was a relief that no one around me bothered about getting everything right all the time.

At the back of my mind, I thought my life was going too well and began to dread the moment when everything would disintegrate. I had not been used to this kind of stability since my boarding school years. I feared an ultimate collapse, so rather than wait, I created one. I quit my job and went to

Switzerland to study French and work with my uncle, who was then Ghana's Ambassador to the United Nations and Switzerland. On a summer day, I boarded the night train to Geneva. As soon as I arrived, I moved in with my cousin *Dzagble* in her studio apartment and traveled to Bern to see my uncle. Everything went well, but I was bored and began reminiscing about the disciplined, comfortable life I had left back home. I remembered that I had made a conscious decision to make it on my own, and realized that I did not want a free ride.

All summer I yearned for the noise and romance of Rome. I missed Bruno terribly. I missed our afternoon conversations when we discussed our daily lives. We had talked a few times, but not frequently due to the expense. So I finished my course and headed back to Rome with an understanding that my uncle would supplement my income until I was back on my feet.

While I was in Geneva, I had encouraged Bruno to go to England to work and study at his company's headquarters. It would mean a promotion for him when he came back to Rome. We were separated for over a year, but he came to see me whenever he visited his parents for a few days. These short interludes were not enough to restore the romantic life we had enjoyed, and we decided to date other people. My heart was not into dating, so I stayed single. I didn't mind being alone, but I felt that I had sabotaged the best relationship I'd ever had. I realized that I never once told Bruno how I truly felt about him, although everyone else knew. I had found the romantic, emotional and intellectual relationship I had come to Rome for, and I had pushed it away. Most of my African friends at the Embassy had objected to my dating a white man and made no attempt to hide their disappointment. They believed that women were more vulnerable to giving away political secrets in an interracial relationship than men were. Of course, I disagreed because there was no proof or fact behind this point of view.

I started working at the Ghana Embassy. I understood the ramifications of putting myself back into the lives of people I had avoided. The counselor who had dropped me off that first Christmas in the middle of nowhere still worked there, and he still had not found the value in apologizing. At this point, I realized he was not worth acknowledging.

On the flip side and while working with Ghana's delegation to the 21st UNFAO Conference, we received an invitation to the Vatican to meet His Holiness Pope John Paul II in his private chapel. As he shook my hand, he asked me where I came from. I answered "Ghana." He said with a beautiful smile and a sparkle in his eye, "I have been to your country." He continued holding my hand in his left hand and extended his right hand to the next person, and continued sharing his experience on that journey. It was a brief moment but it stands out as one of the most privileged experiences in my life. His heart was so open it was impossible not to feel his radiance. I was even luckier when I received a photograph, a recording of this moment.

Besides this gracious encounter, I made a concerted effort to continue my life without further entanglements. This was successful until I started dating again, this time with a married Ghanaian who was thirty-three years my senior. It was a cultural norm and I had no inhibitions except to process it internally against my own moral standards. I only craved security and stability. *Horatio* was experiencing his mid-life crises, while trying to avoid his feelings about it. Our relationship was both boring and complicated. We did not do fun things, socialize, and go to movies or dances. He split his time, resources and emotions between two women but expected one hundred percent commitment from me. I was caught in a relationship that was based on an old antiquated idea that the man is the only head of the home and free to make decisions without consulting his wife.

One afternoon, I told Horatio that if Bruno walked through the door I would not hesitate to leave. This brought up a discussion about marriage. I dared him to propose to me, and he did, only because he was afraid that I would leave him for Bruno. I sobbed at the thought that I had left home to infuse passion into my life, and here I was accepting the most casual, unromantic, and egotistic proposal. And it was all because of my need for stability!

The more promises *Horatio* made about the future, the more I challenged him. If he said we would go on a vacation next year, I demanded that we go now or he withdraw the offer because several of his promises never materialized. My behavior did not discourage him. He went ahead with the traditional "door knocking" ceremony and asked my uncles for permission to request my hand in marriage. In this ceremony, he expressed his intentions formally to my family. Before consent was usually given, an informal investigation was conducted to determine whether the groom-to-be came from a noble or descent family.

We returned to Ghana and the date was set for a face-to-face meeting. It was traditional to investigate a potential husband's background and family history to see if he would be suitable, but *Horatio*'s position as a diplomat was enough to avert any serious investigation. On the appointed date, our two families met and the dowry was paid. After the customary pouring of libation and prayers to the ancestors, the men shared several bottles of gin, and I became *Horatio*'s second wife. My fate was sealed after a few bottles of gin. I felt cheated and belittled.

My oldest uncle had met with *Horatio* privately and received several other gifts, which were shipped directly to him without my knowledge. Now *Horatio* believed he had gone beyond his traditional duty. Because I had challenged him to deliver on his promises, I felt caught in a spiral. I threw several challenges at him hoping that he would give up and leave. He was determined to prove that it was not a game. I felt it would be unfair to walk out even though that would have been the best thing. It was baffling that with the man I loved the most, Bruno, I was unaware of his feelings but with Horatio, I was always aware. Maybe, it was because the relationship felt safer with *Horatio*. It allowed me to avoid intimacy.

The next day *Horatio* took me to his family home in *Saltpond* and introduced me to his aunt as his new wife. As his aunt congratulated me, all I could think of was the difference in our ages. I was only 27, and he was so much older. This was a man who intellectually stimulated me and could provide some security, but had no heart. My life with him lacked any of the romance, sophistication and passion that were important to me. As a second wife, I was going to live a life that would not give me the fulfillment my heart desired. In fact, this relationship was against everything I wanted for myself.

Resigned, I urged myself to be happy for my circumstances, while I silently scolded myself for my failing. On our return to the city, I urged him to take me to my Aunt *Naamele*'s house in Accra. He reminded me that I was his wife now and could not go home to sleep in my own bed anymore. I felt a knot at the pit of my stomach. I had challenged my fate and lost. I felt melancholy but it was a moonlit night and I allowed the light to lift my spirits for the moment. After we made love, I had this strange intuition I had conceived my first child.

Several weeks after our return to Rome, and after the confirmation that I was pregnant, the doctor suggested a change of scenery due to my persistent illness. I was throwing up all the time and could not keep down food or water. I had more than morning sickness, and it was so chronic the doctor prescribed some medications and injections to enable me to consume and hold down fluids.

I decided to take my doctor's advice to change my environment and I moved to Brazil where my first cousin *Dzagble* worked at the Ghana Embassy. As I separated from *Horatio*, I welcomed the freedom to pull my thoughts and emotions together. Of all the places I have visited and lived, including West African Coastal cities, European cities like Rome, Berne, London, Brasilia contrasted the most to any place I have been. The city's streets, apartment buildings and exits were all the same block after block. A planned city, the *superquadras* as it was called, lacked the pristine flair of Switzerland's architecture and the bold, romantic emotions of Rome. It appeared to be a monotonous environment with everything looking the same day after day. What set it apart from all the other places were the spectacular sunsets.

Strangely, I found the monotony of this city to be a blessing in disguise, because I had nothing to distract me from the emotional issues at hand. I focused on my health and my baby. I welcomed the opportunity to address those issues. I walked several miles everyday, reminisced on what could be, and the beautiful sunsets sealed my thoughts. This process brought some sense of peace.

Five months later, my daughter Minty was born. Oh, what a gift! As I looked at her magnificence, I appreciated and bonded with a higher power. At the time, I was not practicing anything spiritually uplifting, but I quietly thought of the possibilities that I might one day understand how it came to be that Spirit bestowed on me such wonderful experiences in spite of my shortcomings. This thought was quickly relegated to the back of my mind. *Horatio* had ordered that I go back to Ghana to live with my mother. I went against his wishes and decided to rejoin him in Rome, because I could not fathom the reasoning behind that request. I felt there was more to it than was presented.

My return to Rome was not pleasant. *Horatio* was angry because I had refused to go home to live with my mother as he had ordered. The knowledge that I had disobeyed his orders bruised his ego and brought on unreasonable tirades. He was my "Svengali", dictating my every move without giving any consideration to my feelings. Here I was with my first child, and the thought foremost on my mind was to share the awe that I felt with her father before anything else.

He, on the other hand, had arranged to have his daughter's naming ceremony performed in Ghana before he had even seen her. For him, following tradition was more important than the emotional adjustment he needed to make. In addition, I had not lived with my mother since I turned 17. I was now 28, and going back home was the last place I wanted to be. From the time of my unusual union, my mother had not answered any of my letters, nor did I receive any information about what upset her so.

I felt mother was deeply disillusioned. I interpreted her silence as a sign of disappointment. She thought I could have made a better choice that could have brought me a more dignified existence. Deep down I knew she was right, but in my mind at the time, that existence could not be guaranteed in any shape or form since most marriages were defined along the same lines as I was in. It was a miserable revolving door for the wives, concubines and female acquaintances. In my case, I had half-heartedly entered the relationship knowing full well what could happen, but I had not bargained for the total disregard for my feelings as a new mother by *Horatio*.

For several months *Horatio* and I continued to argue. I wanted to go back to work, but he said, "No!" He even went as far as telling an interviewer that I did not have the skills required for a job for which I had applied with one of the UN organizations. He did not want me to work, yet he was unwilling to provide enough money for me to make other plans. I had to ask for everything, and he made sure it was a painstaking process. Slowly my respect for him, and myself, diminished.

I could not bear for him to touch me, and each month that went by without sex gave him the excuse to tighten his squeeze and control my life. At some point he refused to provide money, even for food. I was appalled by his cruelty, and knowing that he slept soundly in spite of the way he treated me made me dislike him all the more. As the situation worsened, my best friend, Mara, and I concluded that the easiest way out of the impasse was for me to reconsider my determination not to have sex. Our strategy worked. I would give in to his sexual advances, and the next day he would be generous and kind.

My willingness to prostitute my way out of the relationship made me incredibly sad. For the first time in my life, I lay next to someone I could not love. The only way I could live with my actions was to remember my love for my daughter. Meanwhile, I developed a plan to escape this tumultuous relationship. I joined my older sister, *Essumanba,* in the United States. The Ghana Ambassador, a family friend, and Mowbray Nicholas, one of the Directors at the United Nations, whom I had met earlier in Rome, intervened on my behalf by talking with *Horatio*. With the support of these powerful men and my sister, I didn't feel so alone. Now there was little *Horatio* could do to stop me from leaving.

One day Bruno called just "out of the blue" to see how I was doing. I told him about Minty and what was going on in my relationship. Like a dashing prince in a romantic novel, he came to the rescue. He called daily to find out how we were doing. He took us occasionally to the park and to other activities in town so that Minty could play with other kids. His support strengthened me through those challenging times. He arranged for the shipment of the few things I needed to bring with me to the United States. All my other belongings would be given away, and in order not to arouse suspicion, my friend Angela would distribute everything after I left.

During yet another argument, I told *Horatio* of my impending departure. He was so stunned he could not disguise his feelings, although he tried. He believed that he had taken control of the situation and nipped my feminist attitude in the bud. Ghanaian women were supposed to be submissive to men, especially in marriage, and he truly believed that his cruelty had forced me to accept that role. He was wrong. I found the strength to leave.

I remember an incident that happened shortly before I left for the United States. I had gone to the grocery to pick up some items that *Horatio* and his brother had requested for dinner. By the time I came back, Minty had soiled her diaper. Rather than change her, they had sat there waiting for me to return. As soon as I walked through the door, *Horatio* told me to get my daughter cleaned up. I gave him a choice to either start dinner or clean her up himself. I could see the shock in his brother's face. No traditional Ghanaian wife would ever talk to her husband that way, but I didn't care. I could see a flash of anger on my brother-in-law's face and Horatio sat with a stony face, embarrassed.

By now I had siphoned enough money to pay for all my travel expenses with three hundred dollars to spare. Rather than dwell on the failure of this relationship, I focused on my love for my daughter and the new life that I would build for us in the United States. On the day of our departure, I made *Horatio* take us to the airport!

CHAPTER 5
The Transition

Minty and I arrived in Connecticut a couple of days before Thanksgiving 1985. All we had were a few possessions and the three hundred dollars I'd saved. We were thankful for our new beginnings, especially for the support from my sister, *Essumanba*, who graciously opened her home to us. We laughed together and shared a holiday feast of traditional American and Ghanaian food. We had turkey, mashed potatoes, sweet potato pie and mushroom sauce. There were plantains, *kenkey,* fish with *shito,* a fiery sauce of fresh chili peppers with onions and tomatoes; *garri foto,* made with grated and roasted cassava, and *joloff* rice.

I had always wanted to come to the United States. I believed that it was the most progressive culture there was, anywhere. I knew that if I worked hard and persevered, I would have the life of freedom and expression I wanted. Before long, I realized just how unprepared I was for the differences between my expectations and reality. Most of my ideas about the United States were based on images of popular culture I had seen in Africa and Europe. In political news, I often heard the expression of outrage about human rights abuses around the world. The most impressionable images were presented in movies where city skylines, fancy clothing and boisterous attitudes prevailed. There were no hints of ghettos, racism, segregation and or injustice nor did I imagine people living without running water, or electricity as was the case in rural areas in the developing world.

I expected everyone to love everyone else. The racism and stereotyping I encountered were shocking and often disrupted the peaceful flow of positive energy in my life. When I was in Rome, I lived in an all-white community. No one ever made me uncomfortable. If anything, they did not hesitate to tell me how beautiful I was. "*Sei una bella donna*" or "*que bella*", I heard often and knew it was said from the heart. Then I came to the United States and was followed by a store clerk who assumed I was there to steal!

Another surprise was the use of foul language. Never had I seen such public displays of profanity. It also troubled me that I encountered such lack of sincerity when people greeted or acknowledged each other. In Ghana, if someone wanted to know how I was doing, they would stop everything they were doing and give me their undivided attention.

I remember how as children we delivered messages to the elders in the community.

"Good morning, *Maame Adom*," we would say. "My grandmother asked me to come and wish you a good day and find out whether you slept well last night. She also wants me to apologize for not coming here in person, but she woke up with a slight pain in her hip and cannot make the walk. However, she wants me to convey her sincere gratitude for the fruits you sent to her, which were delicious. She wants you to know that when the cock crows in the morning it carries her voice of gratitude."

Maame Adom would then respond, "Please tell your grandmother that by God's grace, I am well and slept well last night. The fruits were from our farm and I am pleased that she enjoyed them. Please tell your grandmother that with her permission, I will stop by this evening before supper to see how she is doing."

In America, a person doesn't break stride as she walks by hurriedly saying, "Hi! How are ya?"

Before the response is delivered, "Wonderful! Have a nice day! Thanks!" the people are separated by several yards. There's been no eye contact; no expression of genuine interest, and neither one is really sure how the other is feeling. It felt awkward when people walked past me without a greeting but it was especially strange to receive a mechanical greeting.

After a few months, I moved into my own apartment. For the next year, I worked in my brother-in-law's internal medicine clinic as the office manager. After that I held various positions in the insurance industry. I poured my heart and soul into my work and into raising Minty. There was little room for anything else. A friend of mine did introduce me to a man.

She thought it was unhealthy for me to be going without male friendship for so long, so she arranged for me to meet a guy she knew and thought I would like. He was slender and well-dressed, but when he pleasantly smiled at me, I noticed that most of his front teeth were missing. I wondered what possessed my friend and never saw the young man again.

Adapting to American culture was a continual challenge. Privacy is guarded and respected in Ghanaian culture. Americans seemed to talk so openly about everything that happened in their homes and with their families, I was stunned. I believed in sharing, but some of the details were quite embarrassing. People I hardly knew divulged very personal health issues, most of which I did not want to hear or know about. From my point of view, people who were so careless about sharing the details of their lives or chose to divulge every detail could not be trusted to keep others' confidences, so I consciously chose to keep the details of my life to myself.

I continued to focus on my career. I was not aggressive, but took advantage of opportunities that opened up. I started as a secretary, taught myself computer software programs and was promoted several times to higher levels, even to the executive wing of the company, receiving bonuses yearly. Within the office, I established relationships that required a minimal emotional investment. I also became a graphic designer and opened my own business. Having my sister nearby made it easier for me to work so hard. On the weekends, Minty would go to my sister's home and play with her cousins, while I learned new software programs or worked.

In fact, I had developed the attitude of a super woman, juggling two to three jobs, socializing and behaving like a goddess for everyone else. My goal was to work my way back to the lifestyle I had enjoyed in Rome and in Ghana. I wanted to buy a home of my own and provide a good education for my daughter. I was not concerned about my personal difficulties, or happiness, and was not motivated to examine my feelings.

But the human mind, body and spirit will be ignored for only so long. By my tenth year in Connecticut, my carefully constructed life began to unravel when I received an average performance review at work. What most people would take in stride was for me an attack on my personal integrity. I could not believe that anything I did was mediocre. Mediocre performance did not require much effort in my opinion, and I had worked myself to near exhaustion that year. It was also unimaginable to me that someone who talked to me, smiled at me and sometimes brought me lunch could be hiding such deep reservations about my ability. I felt betrayed and lied to.

For almost a year I tortured myself over the situation. I felt desperate and unsettled. One night I dreamed that I had fallen asleep behind the wheel of my car and smashed into a concrete wall. Luckily, I recognized that the dream was a signal that I needed to talk to someone, and with the help of the employee benefits counselor, I decided to see a psychologist.

Talking about my personal life with an outsider was a huge departure from the code of privacy I had brought with me from Ghana, and that worried me. I was also concerned about expressing my beliefs and indigenous practices to an American who would have had no formal training in incorporating them into western medical practices. But I was determined to do whatever was necessary to stay sane.

During the course of my discussions with the psychologist, I decided that going home to Ghana would be the best cure for me at that time. I needed to feel a connection to my roots and something tangible. I wanted to be in a familiar and secure environment. Even though I had dealt with some of the anger and humiliation I felt after my review, I still wasn't comfortable with much of my life in the United States because some people went out of their way to deny me that sense of belonging. Sometimes it was just difficult to assimilate the old values with the new. Also, the psychologist and I were tiptoeing around some subjects I did not feel comfortable discussing.

I noticed during this time that I had lost touch with my achievements, goals and hopes; but most importantly, I lost sight of my confidence and fearlessness. I often stayed awake all night, unable to think of one thing I had accomplished that day that could make me proud. Sometimes I would find solace in a drink. I desired the company of a lover, yet I did not feel beautiful enough to be touched. I would hug my little girl, but I did not remind her very often how precious she was to me. I cried in my sleep. Just going through the day's normal activities was agony. I thought about death.

I often thought of my father, believing that he was turning in his grave worrying about me. This was the second time in my adult life I thought of my dad. The first was after my rape when I was distraught. Seeing my dad, or thinking about him, showed the depth of the despair I felt in that moment in time.

I felt that going home would help me solve these problems. The dignity of my name, ancestors, heart and soul would be reenergized by familiar surroundings, songs and relationships. But I recognized that my connections to Ghana were tenuous. I hadn't completely forgotten the reason I'd left. And I knew my grandmother's warmth would not be there to comfort me. Still, Ghana was my homeland. I took a month's vacation from work and booked a flight for Minty and I.

My heart jumped as I stepped off the plane in Accra. As we drove towards my mother's home, I could feel the rhythm of hi-life blaring all around. Everything felt so close, the breeze from the ocean and the taste of the fruit. I felt my ancestors calmly welcome me. The city had changed little since my last visit.

As I walked through the gates of the familiar compound, I heard my mother say *"Maame Esi oooooo!"* I responded *"Auntie oooooo! Atuuuuu."* Her warm welcome embraced me and any questions I'd had about returning were washed away. For several days we talked pleasantly, catching up on the news since my last visit. I discussed everything else but my emotional state. I never sensed a perfect time to start the conversation. My mother never asked and neither did anyone else.

This situation presented a real dichotomy. On the one hand, beginning with my boarding school years, and as was the norm with her peers, my mother and I had not found a connection to discussing anything deeply personal, intimate and emotional. On the other, I arrived home with suitcases full of gifts, money and very nice clothes. No one in that environment would associate any hardships to the visible affluence.

It still would have been nice to have someone, especially a close relative, ask how I was faring. Unfortunately, some people had the illusion that because I had lived abroad I was a millionaire, and could provide gifts without limits. They were more ˜worried about what I'd brought them than they were about why I'd returned. There was no way to describe the pain and disappointment I felt. Emotionally, I was distraught in ways I could not understand or clarify. The consolation I'd sought was out of reach and knowing that left me feeling strangely disconnected. After the warmth and pleasant days with my mother, I believed that I had no one else I could turn to in my despair. Soon, it was time to return to the United States.

Minty and I walked hurriedly through customs to board the plane. As we approached the gate there was yet another security checkpoint. The men were ordered to stand in the line on the left side and women to the right. I was first in line. After some questions about my final destination, how much money I had and how much I could give in tips, one of the female customs officers reached out unexpectedly and touched my breasts. There was no warning about a body search. I was alarmed and yelped in surprise. The *obroni* woman standing behind us with her two teenagers looked very surprised also. My reaction amused the kids including my daughter. I was actually grateful for the distraction caused by the kids because it enabled me to concentrate on the bizarre airport security routine instead of my emotional state. The gratitude for this distraction underlined the continued disconnection to the more pressing issues in my life.

When we arrived at JFK, a heavy snow was falling with freezing temperatures as is usual with Nor'easters. By the time we got home, Minty and I were both sick from whatever we ate at the airport restaurant in Amsterdam. Exhaustion and jet lag set in very quickly, and surprisingly, I was glad to be back to the place I had so recently tried to escape. We snuggled and found comfort in our own beds.

After a few days of rest, I decided that a heavy work schedule and a last minute shopping spree were the best ways to drown some of my pain and disappointments. On the way back to the car from shopping, I slipped on ice and wrenched my back. What I suspected to be just a muscle pull turned out to be a spinal injury.

I showed up at work the next morning limping slightly and after a couple of hours at my desk, I called our Health Services nurse and told her about the discomfort, which seemed to be getting worse. I was advised to take Ibuprofen and see how I felt. By late afternoon, I could not get up from my chair. Security moved me in a wheel chair and my sister came to pick me up. I opted for a ride with my sister instead of the ride on an ambulance. I found the latter option to be too traumatic. I still underestimated the extent of my injury and avoided the hospital visit that day. I assumed the painkillers would rectify the situation by morning.

That night I crawled on all fours just to get to the bathroom. It took me almost half an hour to pull myself off the floor onto the toilet seat. Sitting on the seat was another torture. Getting off the seat was another unimaginable hurdle. By the time I managed to get back to my bed, almost an hour had passed for something that should have taken a couple of minutes. The pain was increasing.

Finally, the ruptured and bulging discs made my spine feel like it had collapsed. The pain was excruciating. I had to see the doctor first thing Monday morning. He prescribed anti-inflammatory drugs and bed rest for the first couple of weeks. While the spasms around the para-spinal muscles improved a little bit, I was still in distress and physical therapy was added to my routine. Traction was used at the onset of my symptoms, but each time the heavy cast weights were released, my spine collapsed into a tangled mess. I wished for a warm traditional wrap of wide, roasted banana leaves with herbs, instead of this high-tech treatment.

During the course of my initial physical rehabilitation, I tried to continue with life as if nothing had happened. With the help of heavy doses of prescription painkillers, including Vicodin, I limped my way through the next eighteen months, hoping that keeping almost the same level of activity would make the problem go away, but it persisted. Occasionally, I would get a little better and think that things were getting back to normal. These respites never lasted. The simplest accomplishments required Herculean efforts. I spent a lot of time at physical therapy. I could not sit for long, so I avoided social engagements.

At work, the prescription drugs slowed me down both physically and mentally, so I quit taking them during the day, clenching my teeth against the pain. At night I would take the prescribed dosage, trying to make up for lost time. Soon my dreams turned into nightmares, and I would lay awake most of the night afraid to go back to sleep. Each time I closed my eyes, a freshly dug grave appeared with me standing next to it as an unidentified person tried hard to push me in. Most of the time I would resist, but there were times when I felt like simply giving in. Sometimes my dreams would shift subtly. Family members would welcome me to functions they were hosting, and I would feel happy. It was only after I awoke that I realized the relatives I dreamt about were all dead.

About a year and a half after I became injured, the doctors scheduled me for back surgery. The Saturday before, I decided to pick up a friend and head to the Chinese store to purchase some jasmine rice, soy sauce and other ingredients for my homemade fried rice. We stopped to buy pizza for Minty, and my friend promised to cook lunch the next time we visited. But just as the statement about our next visit came out of his mouth, a dark voice that only I could hear, instructed me to tell him that this was the last time he was going to see me. I would not come out of the back surgery alive. My heart was pounding so fast I thought I would explode.

I didn't show my emotions outwardly, but under my very cool exterior, I was caught in the grip of a deep struggle. On one side were the dreams and this sinister voice telling me I was going to die. On the other was a flicker of hope that I simply wouldn't surrender. Not so much because I was afraid of dying, [although maybe I was] but because I just knew that this was not the right time. Often it was hard to know which side was winning. I started putting my affairs in order without being obvious about it. One day I went ahead and arranged for my daughter to attend one of the best schools in the area. I hoped that by continuing to live like nothing was happening, I would be able to overcome the pain and stress I was under.

Two days prior to my surgery, my sister invited me to her church for a Monday morning prayer service. All weekend, I struggled with the idea of going. I had doubts that it would do any good; nothing had worked so far. The dark voice was telling me to call my sister and tell her to pray for me, and that would have the same effect as the service. I realized that the voice belonged to a sort of being that felt uncomfortable with the idea of going to a church. I didn't know what to do.

Monday morning came, and I prepared to run what could be my last errand, rather than go to the prayer service. During the ride, however, I impulsively changed directions and drove to the church. I had no idea what I was doing, but when I walked inside, I felt like I had entered a sanctuary. It seemed I could feel the dark voice's discomfort and felt that perhaps I was gaining some power over it. I also was aware that this could be my last chance to make a plea to God that if it were time for me to pass over, I would be given the strength to deal with it.

The service started on time. After a few songs of praise, the members offered to say a special prayer for me. I knelt down, slumped with excruciating pain. Everyone laid their hands on me. During the prayer, I felt one of the parishioner's hands emit some heat. Then, it was as if some force were trying to move the hand away from my back or keep it there. I wasn't sure which. The woman praying for me kept her hand where it was, and leaped a few times, as if she were in a trance, or moved by Spirit.

Some minutes into the prayer, I saw a bright light and a very reassuring voice told me not to slouch but rather to hold myself up. I was told in no uncertain terms that I had nothing to be afraid of. My eyes were closed, but I could see clearly, as if the ceiling had opened and a light shone from the sky. There was a figure in the center of the light. Surprised by what was unfolding, I was drawn into the energizing light. It was like nothing I could have imagined. Most importantly, this was my very first experience of having a direct exposure to something holy and powerful. At that moment, a dark shadow, whose origins I did not care to know, moved away from my body. The warm hand on my back cooled down, and I breathed a sigh of relief. I was filled and surrounded by a feeling of pure love and joy.

I had a couple of days to bask in the new energy before I reported for surgery. As we approached the operating room, the anesthesiologist commented, without humor, that back surgery was not a picnic. He was right. When I came out of surgery, the pain was worse than it had been when I went in.

I looked and felt awful. My right leg was totally numb with an adhered nerve root. The assurances from the surgeon that things would change did not come true. I was in such bad shape even showering was difficult. During this time, Minty helped a great deal. She helped me bathe and put on lotion, underwear, clothes and shoes. She also did the laundry and cooked. I don't know where she gained the strength to handle all the changes.

She learned to deal with many difficult tasks around the house and I agonized about having her play such an adult role at such a young age. She was 11. Our once spontaneous life full of fun and jokes had regressed to one of dependency.

It pained me a great deal to know that she was hiding her own fears about my deteriorated health and was choosing to present a tough front. I did not have such responsibilities at her age and would not have had to take them on due to the intervention of adults in the community. Although I had a lot of support, she still had plenty to do and she did it all beautifully and without complaints.

After the surgery, I fell down several times as I practiced moving my leg. Sometimes it would just give out without warning. On a trip to the pharmacist's, I tried to hold on to a shelf to keep from falling and knocked down a whole display in the process. Some bystanders helped me up, and I limped my way out, frustrated and embarrassed. To get into a chair or into the car, I had to lift my leg off the floor and drop it into place. Every fall and every move was agony. I could not drive anymore. For three years, my right leg remained like wood and thumped heavily when I walked. It was extremely painful to move, but I was so determined to walk again, I valued the few minutes of walking as a blessing. For someone who had never had any major illness, all of this was inexplicable.

Emotionally, mentally and spiritually I was exhausted. I worked hard to regain my physical strength, religiously performing assigned exercises while the tears streamed down my face. When my surgeon told me that there was little chance of further improvement, I worked harder. I believed that he did not have the final say. That was between Spirit and me.

I started going to a healing service at the invitation of my dear friend Carol. Carol was one of those friends I did not have to explain anything to or ask for anything. She had a big heart, and with it, she did wonderful things for others. We first met at work and she later became my boss. She was a delight to work for, and even though I had this hands-off attitude with friendship at the workplace, she always went out of her way to make sure I had everything I needed to do my job.

She was especially supportive of my physical therapy and visits to doctors before the surgery. Getting time off was never an issue. She was my first colleague in this country who felt comfortable enough to invite me to her home for dinner and several others since. She proved in so many ways that she loved me unconditionally. She never once expected anything in return. She did all she could do to make my disrupted life better, and I love her dearly for it.

Unfortunately, I could not say the same for other friends who tormented me about my weight gain, or my inability to bite through the pain and look strong. Some of them even commented on Minty's sullen and worried mood. She had just turned ten when I got injured, and was eleven and a half when I had my surgery. Too often, words of 'critical support' were offered, undermining my confidence and self-esteem. Even though I was bothered by some people's lack of compassion, I chose not to spend too much energy fighting it. I had more pressing issues with which to deal.

During the year after my surgery I felt very ill. I started seeing *Mammi* in my dreams. One night a young man on a fancy bicycle showed up. He looked like my cousin Red and had a goatee. I stared intently for a while and just before I asked who he was, I recognized him. It was *Papa Nii*. Even in death, he still had style. I apologized for not recognizing him sooner. He told me that he came by to let me know that he was close by should I ever need anything.

The visit from grandpa and the more frequent sights of *Mammi* in my dreams were consoling. I realized that I was not alone at the ancestral level and that was significant. My strong relationship with them in real life, and their concern for my well-being from the spirit world boosted the additional support I was receiving on a physical level.

During my childhood and story-telling sessions, I heard many stories about the role our ancestors played in our lives. I was living that experience, and it was humbling to realize how that wisdom had filtered into my life. It was powerful.

CHAPTER 6

New Beginnings

With everything I had been through, I realized that I could not rely on old ways of thinking to solving current problems. I had to start a new process. I began to look at my collapsed physical, emotional and spiritual life for answers. I thought of the muscle spasms as the cries of repressed memories and feelings. The people who could not support me fell away. The supportive ones remained and became a source of strength during my journey. Through them I was offered alternative sources of learning and healing.

The first few weeks of physical therapy after the surgery were a struggle. I remember being asked to ride the stationery bike, but a fresh spinal wound and a numb leg made it impossible to pedal. It turned out that those sessions did more harm than good. I was urged to look in the yellow pages for a new physical therapist. I did, and after a quick glance, without much thought to the history of the organization, I made my decision, and intuition played a significant role in that choice.

I knew upon my arrival at the facility that I was at the right place. It turned out that I'd been led to one of the best physical therapists in town. Miss Shirl was a tall woman with natural blonde hair, as she's quick to tell everyone. She had a quick wit and was extremely hard working. Her approach to healing was tough because she believed that the individual had absolute control over the extent to which they improved, that she was just a medium who moved the process along. She got frustrated when a patient did not take the assigned exercises seriously and would reschedule those sessions under direct supervision if necessary. I found it was easier to do the homework. Shirl recommended therapeutic massage, herbal treatments and aquatic therapy, which I did even though I didn't know how to swim and was afraid of the water.

There was only a modicum of improvement over a long period of time. But I stuck with the routine even after discharge from physical therapy and noticed that the regimen really worked. I had begun walking without my cane, but the pain in my back and numbness in my right leg persisted.

Shirl had made a personal commitment to seeing me recover and became a source of support in my life, even though we disagreed on some issues, mostly political. On Mother's Day after my surgery, I could not drive and had been stressed because my daughter and I could not do anything together. At about five in the evening, my doorbell rang and there was

Shirl with dinner for Minty and me.

It would be unfair if I left out some of my friends, who have stood by me through it all – I would leave my daughter with the McCaulleys any day, because they had an incredible capacity to love unconditionally. My friend Sam allowed me some foolishness. Sam is about five feet nine inches tall, medium build and sported an afro hairdo. He is a very quiet *Ghanaman*. He did not talk much, but every now and then, he presented a spark of interest and energy that could be surprising. I have never known Sam to betray a confidence. His gentle demeanor made him an easy target for some teasing, which I have enjoyed. In addition to another friend, Oseh, Sam had played the role of a surrogate father for Minty.

My massage therapist was one of the most supportive people in my life. When I met Kyle, he reminded me of one of my dearest friends, the late Reverend Abioseh Cole. Oseh, as we called him, was the pastor at the local Methodist Church, where my sister was a member. A native of Sierra Leone, he was also President of the African Affairs Association. Kyle's gentleness and nonjudgmental attitude were a comfort during those tiresome times. In fact, he was at the top of my list of people who taught me about friendship. As a good friend he recognized both my strengths and weaknesses and knew exactly how to use both to help me through difficult and good times. He unselfishly and honestly gave his time, wisdom and other resources to improve my life.

Overall, I was learning to come to terms with my limitations, which was very difficult. My recovery was proceeding slowly, and without faulting anyone, I could not grasp why so. Friends from Ghana even suggested that a witch involved. But why would a witch be interested in me? There was nothing to gain from my already broken spirit. I even challenged more logical suggestions that I needed to be patient and rest more.

My know-it-all attitude sometimes hindered my recovery. The more I rushed to get better, the more circumstances forced me to settle down and accept my new limitations. All my old belief systems and defenses were under assault. In order to find some equilibrium, it was imperative that I keep an open mind to trying new things.

On one occasion, someone mentioned trying acupuncture. Then two more people I did not know brought up the subject. I felt like I was getting a message. The decision to do acupuncture was a difficult one because I did not like needles. I thought, however, that I had managed to overcome my fear of swimming. I could overcome this one too.

The determination to forge ahead matched my desire to heal permanently. I made an appointment to see Richard Moon, a Korean acupuncturist. When I arrived at his office, just before I opened the door to his suite, I could smell the strong aroma of herbs in the hallway. His wife pleasantly greeted me and after filling out some paperwork, she escorted me to meet Richard. It was a bright office space and on the walls of his office hung a huge picture of the human anatomy with deep red lines and dots highlighting the pathways called the meridians. He took the time to explain the disruption of 'qi' after surgery. I was persuaded the treatment would help after the initial consultation. Three times a week, I endured the unthinkable as the needles were attached to electrical stimulation for deeper penetration. At some point, he suggested combining the treatment with herbs to get rid of the "dampness". It was a reasonable suggestion, since I was used to herbal treatments in Ghana.

When I brought the mixture home to boil as instructed, my stomach turned at the smell. I opened the windows and lit several candles to help soften the odor. After a few hours, the concoction was ready. The muddy dark greenish liquid was even more difficult to look at, much less drink. But I was not ready to back out, so I poured some into a glass and stared at it while plotting the strategy to get it down my throat. The easiest way was to gulp it down fast, without breathing. I screamed after I emptied the glass – my face contorted to extremes. One day, I just could not hold the liquid down and I knew that was the last straw. Even in the face of challenges, there had to be a limit to things one would do and this was it for me. I continued with the acupuncture for several months, and I noticed that my ability to walk and sit improved.

An interesting pattern was also emerging. From the time I changed physical therapists to the treatment of acupuncture, I felt I was guided to the various things I needed to do to get well. It was subtle but present, and it empowered me to trust my intuition. I also closely examined all my activities and relationships and quit accepting social engagements just because I thought I should. Anything that did not contribute positive energy to my healing was not allowed in my life for very long.

My contact with Spirit during the church visit before my surgery held me together during this time. My prayers always

ntered on the need for Spirit to heal my sore back and restore
the busy me to my old self. The insurance company was taking
its sweet time qualifying me for disability payments. Now
a quarter looked like a fortune. On Thanksgiving, twelve
years to the day after I arrived in the United States, I could
not afford a turkey.

Desperation was setting in. I was both angry and sad when I
saw the fear in my daughter's eyes, quietly asking what we were
going to do. I had to call Sam who worked at the Department
of Children and Families to ask if we were entitled to receive
some food for the holidays. He brought us some canned food
and a turkey. That evening, I sat in my bathroom and cried.
I stared at the blank tiles on the floor, wondering what could
have brought me to where I was.

That night, in my dream, I saw children who had died of
hunger and war and heard their cries. I wept with them and
my pillow was soaked when I woke up. Desperate, I lashed
out at the only source that had given me hope and comfort.
I told God exactly what was on my mind. My previous life,
even though it was flawed at the spiritual level, had never left
me this vulnerable and helpless. If I were to stay committed to
healing and keep an open mind, then I would need additional
support, anything that would bring me some peace and help
solidify my new beliefs and attitude.

If the only proof of a person's spirituality was the number
of times they went to church, I figured there was no hope of
salvation for me. My Christian friends and family had told
me that all my life too. The issues I had with religion made
me a spiritual dabbler with an excuse to worship solo. I had

never understood the African proverb that "a wis
by caravan in the desert of life, while the fool pr
alone." Was I a fool? I was not ready to admit that. Perhaps
I had not found a comfortable medium in which to express
my beliefs. But I understood the concept of fellowship with
others as long as I didn't have to sacrifice my principles in
order to belong to a group.

Trying to keep an open mind, I went to the Episcopal
Church one day and asked Father Wagner who ministered
the weekly healing service, if I could go in alone. He obliged.
I stood in front of the altar and wept. I talked to God. I got
angry and I implored. After venting, I walked out with some
sense of relief because I had said exactly what was on my mind
and how I felt. I also knew that the focus on negative emotions
would lead to false realities. I needed to develop inner strength
during these challenging times to make my new realities pur-
poseful and meaningful. I decided to take a new approach by
learning how to do an introspective analysis of my life.

I joined a meditation class guided by an experienced prac-
titioner and was forced to look into all my relationships,
including family. Through this practice, I realized how much
of my personal power had been compromised and what I
needed to do was take it back. I had to stick to meditation.
So far it had brought me some peace and space to realize what
was at stake. I had learned that the condition of my body was
the direct result of many unresolved problems. If I were to
solve some of those problems, I would have to take seriously
the work of learning to balance my emotions and quiet my
mind before I could embark on a spiritual path.

I found a cherished space in my home. And with my car now fitted with hand controls, I had no excuse for not finding one outdoors. I spun my way one day to one of the most peaceful and beautiful places near my home, Elizabeth Park. I found it extremely difficult to move around alone. On my first day there, I could barely move, but forced myself to take a few steps, and the fresh air did some good.

Even though I did not ask with any expressed intent, my dreams delivered a special message several nights in a row. In these dreams, I was dressed up, wearing a hat with roses on it. In my arms was a dog wearing a matching hat. My first response was to dismiss the possibility of that ever happening. I had yet to meet a Ghanaian man or woman who would carry a dog wearing a matching hat. In the next dream, I saw myself at a dog show, spending an afternoon enjoying the different runs by the competitors and the various grooming styles. I was equally doubtful that I would ever do that. I had never seen a dog show prior to coming to the United States, so the idea of attending one seemed very odd to me.

These dreams continued for several more nights then stopped. About a week later, my daughter's best friend called to say there was a dog that would be put to sleep if the owner did not find a new home for him. Saddened by what I heard, I immediately offered to take the dog. After days of thinking about it, I tried to get out of my commitment, because I had not had a pet before and did not know whether I had what it took to take care of one. It seemed that fate would not have any of it. I made an appointment to go see the dog, and while it rolled on its back, I made another excuse to come back and pick him up later. The owner ignored my gentle protest and opened my car door. My new friend, Rocky, without hesitation, jumped in.

Rocky and I drove off together. He jumped over my head a few times during our trip to the vet's and then to school to pick up Minty. He was badly in need of grooming, so I spent the evening with my yellow pages until I found a shop that would take him first thing in the morning. When I picked him up, he had a bandana around his neck and a swagger in his step. It was worth every cent of the thirty-five dollars I spent. I could not let Rocky spend one more night dirty and unclipped. I also believed that because Rocky was sent my way from the spirit world, I would get financial help with whatever money I needed to care for him. We all managed to get by that month.

Now I had a companion for my walks in the park. One day at a time, with a lot of tears and laughter, our morning walk became a ritual we both enjoyed regardless of the weather. When I sat down on a bench discouraged, Rocky would come nudge my leg to continue. I would get up and walk to the next bench and he would roll on the grass happy. I cried sometimes because I knew that even the little progress I made had such a profound effect on him. I laughed at his little tricks.

I used each day's visit to meditate and appreciate nature. I enjoyed the peace and my freedom. Each step I took brought hope and I began feeling my presence in nature. I had done this when I was young and related very well to the sounds around me. I was in touch with my heart once again. But I was also learning a lot from Rocky. No matter what the weather conditions were, his mood expressed fully the joy of living in that moment. His attitude was infectious. And as I became more in tune with my environment, I once again heard the childlike voice within my heart and recognized how often the Divine had intervened in my life.

I reflected on my past and present state of affairs. My perceptions about what was important and what was not began to change. Slowly, I became aware of the seasonal changes and the unique beauty of each season. In spring, the trees slowly started budding, the birds chirped and the squirrels scuttled from tree to tree. The season brought new colors and rain. I noticed and floated with the thin clouds as they moved across the light blue sky. I became aware of the cloudy mists and the mood they set on the people that walked by. I appreciated the greetings from strangers and from familiar faces that seemed glad to see me again.

The golden-reddish colors of fall were my favorite. The soft wind would blow the leaves to the ground and it was as if someone held their hands to catch each leaf before it landed. In the winter, as the sun hit the snow at an angle, I saw and admired the jewels that sparkled all around me. For an African woman, I had come a long way to admiring and appreciating the sound and crunch of the powdery snow under my boots.

One of my favorite places in the park was the rose garden where on a typical summer day, the colors and scents mesmerized my senses. Finding silence outdoors and in my heart brought a new awareness and understanding of how to contemplate and deal with my limitations without feeling sorry for myself or being angry. Silence became part of my daily routine. I learned to meditate lying down, walking and listening to music.

What a brave soul my daughter was during this time. Her life was seriously affected by my limitations, but as I became more independent, I found ways to let her spend more time with friends and at after school activities. During the first few months after surgery, she would rise early, get herself ready and help me shower and put on my clothes. One morning she rushed to the kitchen and made breakfast. The eggs and toast were burned, but I ate every morsel and told her how delicious it was. I realized all our mother and daughter cooking sessions were being applied. She later told me that watching me eat that egg that morning was one of the best moments in her life.

The meditation class, my solitary walks in the park, my ability to acknowledge universal suffering and be willing to do something about it brought me an infusion of energy. Something I didn't quite understand was definitely happening. Spiritually and emotionally I was on the move and my previous inertia was being reversed. I was being prodded to look closely into my heart. But why? My heart was fine, or so I thought.

One afternoon, when I was so crippled that I could not get out of the hospital bed in my living room, I fell asleep. I dreamed that I was sleeping but doing everything I could to get up and move. I dressed up in a nice navy blue suit with my portfolio in hand ready to go out to look for a job. My friend Shirl was there, and my daughter walked ahead of me out of the door. Just as I was ready to follow them, I collapsed to the floor. Shirl and Minty walked back into the room after waiting for a few minutes outside. I seemed to be outside of my body watching everything. They tried waking me up. The paramedics arrived to pick me up and with a sudden realization that I may be watching this live from the ceiling, I jammed right back into my body and woke up.

I could not make sense of the dream. I was concerned and confused. I began working with several more healing professionals. I had an astrologer and an herbalist in addition to the massage and physical therapists. Through these consultations, I was beginning to more fully understand that my injury was a direct result and reaction to imbalanced life force energy caused by the emotional trauma, invalidation and denial of self that I had been carrying my entire life. By that acceptance alone, I felt my suffering had become sanctified. A heavy load lifted from my shoulders as my commitment to heal was accepted by Spirit.

One evening after a very powerful Monday night healing service, Father Ed Wagner asked me to come see him on Thursday at eight o'clock in the morning to talk. Even though I was not at all sure what he would want to talk about, I agreed. We saw each other several times and Father Ed gave me new ways to cope with my limitations. I wept almost every time I sat with him, because I felt the depth of pain I had been through and the changes that had occurred in my life. Even though there were new and exciting things happening in my life, I still faced an uncertain and tenuous future.

With a gentle nudge from Father Ed, I recognized the importance and necessity to surrender. At first, I wondered to what I was supposed to surrender. I figured it out after a long contemplation and a dream. One night before turning in, I poured my heart out to Spirit beseeching humbly that *It* take my whole being. When I woke up, I felt the absence of my burdens instantaneously. I had the same problems I'd gone to bed with, but the weight of them had been lifted. For several days, I felt like I lived in paradise with my physical mishaps seeming less threatening. Father Ed noticed the change, and so did a few others who commented that they saw a glow around me. I felt the glow too.

Things were beginning to look up, but I still had some trouble spots. My finances remained in turmoil. I wondered how I would stay afloat yet another month. What I feared the most was losing my home. One night before I went to bed, I hobbled into the dining room, took a pen and paper and started writing down the amount of money I would need to pay my current bills. The total amount included payments for my mortgage, my car, some utilities and fifty dollars for food. I underlined the total of two thousand and two hundred dollars and went to bed. Before I went to sleep, I said a simple prayer, admitting that I needed help and again submitted everything to Spirit. I had begun feeling good about praying; I understood there was a source outside myself, and I did not have to go at it alone.

About mid-morning the following day, I called the bank to check whether I was in the red yet or whether I could manipulate the fifty dollars I had in the account before the last check was presented for payment. After the usual automated prompts, the computerized message blared into my ears "your available balance on November 30 is two thousand, two hundred and seventy-six dollars and zero cents. For more information on this account press...."

Panicking, I hung up the phone. I thought I must have dialed into the wrong account. I called back and this time asked to speak to a customer service representative. When she came on the line, I explained that I had too much money in my account and that they may have deposited someone else's money into mine. But how often do banks make that mistake? And how likely is it that almost the exact amount I scribbled on the paper had been deposited? After putting me on hold, the customer service representative came back and said, "Ma'am, a direct deposit was made into your account yesterday in the amount of...". I was stunned into tears.

For someone who was so tough and hardly ever cried, a trail of tears followed me throughout the day. The money came from a disability payment I was owed. The payment arrived again the next month without writing an itemized bill. I had dwelled on the immediate physical pain; the power plays by insurance companies, legal maneuverings to get disability benefits, the emotional adjustments of dealing with my new limitations; and all the other issues that were unfamiliar. Letting go of all those things, and giving them over to Spirit made me feel good.

Between the healing service and counseling, I found new activities to fill my days with Minty and Rocky always at the center. The reruns of the Golden Girls became my afternoon date, and I found laughter again. New support systems came through several different avenues. I received financial, emotional and spiritual support. I had dreams that presented my ancestral spirit guides, beauty, elegance and truth. I dreamed that I was called to settle a conflict about a house, which had been sold by the original owner to another man. My maternal grandparents were the judges at the table and asked me to write a report on who I thought was telling the truth. The new owner had spent time to redecorate. The living room was painted mint green and there were hieroglyphs on the wall. The former owner, seeing the new condition of the house, tried to get it back. This was an easy decision for me to make. When I presented my report, my grandparents expressed their pleasure and left.

I remained in the house I had just inspected with my daughter who had accompanied me. We settled in the living room on the marbled floor. I was braiding Minty's hair and as we looked up at the ceiling; it became transparent. We could see the sky and the stars. Then I saw a cherub. In the dream I looked away, thinking I was either imagining things or losing my mind. But when I looked up again the sky filled with cherubs. How awesome! The many others I told of my dream drew only one conclusion – the sky was the limit. I could do whatever my heart desired.

There were now new opportunities to rest my painful body. Many of these restful periods took me to dreamland. One night, my closet door to the right popped open and out stepped a magnificent figure! He wore a white tunic with silvery hair and beard. I gasped and clearly said, "Hello God!"

This spiritual being I had called God walked toward me and sat by my bedside. He then spoke in the gentlest of tones. "I know you have been asking to talk to me for a long time. I am here now. What would you like to know?" Without hesitation, I wanted to know why millions of people were caught in deplorable conditions on this planet without knowing how to get out of their situations. I asked about war, poverty, disease, children and death. "Why are so many children dying; of hunger, abuse and war?" I asked. "Death, as you know it, even of children, is never a waste," he replied. Point by point, I got an answer to all my queries. By the end of that conversation, I understood the personal responsibilities we each have in bringing and sharing our gifts with others in our immediate communities and the world. I also knew what it meant to die. For the first time, I thought of death in positive terms. This was a major shift in my reality, especially since my childhood ghost stories had scared me half to death.

The conversation continued most of the night. As it ended, I had a glimpse of how to relate these messages to the workings of my existence. I was imbued with an intense curiosity about my spiritual experiences after meditating and sometimes in my dreams. This encounter and discussion about death proved to be invaluable.

When my only brother died recently, I was able to reconcile his death with what I had been exposed to in my dream and my new reality. I had called home several weeks earlier to find out how my brother was doing after a short illness. I did not get a chance to talk to him, but I was assured he was fine. But as I hung up the phone, my stomach dropped and I knew something was terribly wrong with that message. A few weeks passed and I had a friend visiting. Her son went outside to roller blade and few minutes later, a van pulled up in my driveway and dropped him off. He was bleeding and held his wrist in pain. He had fallen off his skates as he rolled downhill from the house.

As we rushed downstairs to get him, he was frantically crying, and saying he was going to die. My stomach dropped again but it was somehow not connected to what he was saying. After a visit to ER, we settled in and I recommended the movie "Meet Joe Black" which I thought was very good the first time I saw it. The movie seemed slower than usual but we watched halfway through and decided to call it a night. In my dream that night, I heard a voice ask me three times whether I wanted to meet Joe Black. My answer was a definite no since I knew who Joe Black was. Joe Black, in the movie, was Death, and I did not know where I would be taken if I answered in the affirmative.

When we woke up, I felt melancholy for no reason and by mid-afternoon when we decided to watch the second half of the movie, I had tears in my eyes by the time it was over. A few hours later, I got a phone call from home. My cousin Gina asked whether I knew what had happened. Of course I didn't. In fact, I was ready to admonish her for starting the conversation in such a weird way.

She said "*Papa ewuoooo*"! Papa is dead. Her words jabbed and echoed in my ears. I managed to muffle questions. "What?! When?! I was told he was fine"!

The rest of the conversation was almost a blur. He had died earlier on that day, which was just about the time I was having that dream. My body shook and broke down as I explained to my guests what the news was. I had to find my sister. I had forgotten she was out of town. I started calling places she had worked some years ago trying to find her. I even went through my old phone books trying to remember where she could be. It took a few minutes for the confusion to subside. I now had to deal with this reality. My brother and I had been close and he was my protector during my very boisterous childhood. He afforded me every playtime I wanted, especially the unconventional ones that were forbidden for girls. By our teenage years, our roles switched. He returned home from boarding school and was ill often. The thought him dying so young was unbearable.

I could not bring myself to go to his funeral (for fear of sinking into depression). I remembered the conversation in my dream and that allowed me to deal with my emotional state. I was able to reconcile myself to his passing and the cycle of events that made it part of a divine process. I understood what had happened, and even though I could not explain in words the pain I felt, I was consoled knowing that he was in a better place. His presence around me after his death put my old beliefs and superstitions about ghosts to rest.

I also began to feel that "Headlamp" was reemerging and I was more open to acknowledging the new premonitions. I have had many experiences, from visions to dreams, and altered states of consciousness, that opened doors for me to witness an infinite pool of wisdom in the universe. To know that I am part of that pool of wisdom has been the greatest gift.

An experience after a meditation class one evening left me exhilarated. That night in my dreams, I left my body and traveled with three companions – two females and a male – into cosmic space. As we traveled, the two females were on each side of me and the male flew above me. I felt secure and protected. We came to a place where there was some activity, and suddenly a magnificent being arrived. He was introduced to me as Archangel Gabriel. He welcomed me and gave my guides information as to where to take me. He assured me that I would see him again before my journey back home. During the tour, I saw different structures within the universe and they were beyond beautiful. There were gardens with the most gorgeous flowers being cared for by angels. There was music that made every cell in my body float with joy.

Before my journey back home, the two ladies, whom I believe were my guides and healers, told me to hold my right hand to the energy and vibration which was around me and touch my back whenever I was in distress. Those direct instructions helped with my physical healing. This was just one of many astral exposures.

I start my day with an affirmation: "Thy will be done God, not mine. In me and through me, show me what I must do this day and let me be a channel of your blessings to all." This affirmation allowed me to surrender all my needs and desires, which made it easier for me to just be. I could not worry about the things that were out of my control.

I also perform another ritual, which is meant to express confidence in the angelic protection it invokes. This invocation is part of the Banishing Ritual, a preliminary to Kabalistic ritual work. When I did my research on Kabalistic rituals, I came across information that left me humbled, joyfully tearful, quiet, reflective and awed. The banishing ritual, which was recited in Latin originally, was meant to create and stimulate one's psychic abilities. The visualization techniques involved creating the etheric likeness of four archangels: Raphael, Michael, Gabriel and Uriel. There are several more steps, like the visualization of the six-pointed star above the head, which are aspirations of the lower self towards the higher.

I never pondered my journey into the universe and meeting Archangel Gabriel. But the visit could not be accidental either. During my readings, I came across text in Conway's *Magic: An Occult Primer.* He wrote:

> Turning to the east again, he focuses his attention on the Tree of Life, for he is ready to move from Malkuth, the sphere of Earth, to Yesod, which is the silver gateway to the astral world. Yesod is the sphere of the moon, and the name of Gabriel will be the one he gives on approaching the Ishim who guard the gate.

This find not only confirmed my experience in the astral world, I also recognized with astonishment that I was introduced into this experience long before I was aware of the astral plane, journeying, rituals and visions. I received further confirmation of this interaction with Archangel Gabriel in another dream. In that dream, I was getting married and was given a statement to read. It said that Archangel Gabriel would always be close by to protect me. As I hurried through the ceremony I saw the Archangel in a form of light but could still make out his features. What this meant to me was that I had been exposed deeply into the spiritual and transpersonal spheres as an initiation to what was to come. The path was clearly outlined for me and new doors opened as I became willing to advance.

There were difficulties that I encountered on the path of individual growth and development. Personal growth came with its own pleasures and difficulties; each step forward into unfamiliar territory had its dangers. The dangers often involved dealing with separation from familiar things, even old habits and behaviors that can be experienced as a kind of death and rebirth, loneliness and fear. Separation also required me to give up an easier routine for a more demanding, responsible and seemingly difficult life. It often took time to get used to new spiritual, emotional, mental and physical disciplines. Also, developing faith was not an easy process because I learned it did not emanate from spiritual practice alone but from the depth of one's soul. It took time and devotion to develop, and it is what opened the door to high-level revelations. Learning to surrender to a supernatural source was also a big adjustment. That discovery, and my relationship with destiny, whatever it may be, brought forth images and desires from my soul.

It was inspiring sometimes to state with such certainty that I knew what I had to do to be fully engaged on my spiritual journey. I also understood what it meant to hold my thoughts and passions in the outer world, while finding interior ways to nourish my soul. That was simple, really, because that assurance came from within and was established and intensified with continued spiritual commitment and practice. My practices included meditation, aura cleansing, massage, aromatherapies and outdoor activities. Each practice enhanced the peace and joy I experienced daily, and heightened my ability to create some balance in my life.

When I was out of sorts, worried and fearful, I knew that

I'd lost the balance between my conscious and unconscious. Inner work comprising prayers, meditations, dream work, ritual and imagination or visualization helped me restate that balance. Through these practices, I drew on inner strength and resources to resolve inaccurate perceptions and challenges. The alignment of thoughts, emotions and actions heightened my awareness and gave me the chance to tap into the higher parts of myself. Ultimately, I was able to live with enthusiasm and experience the purpose of my journey. Because my heart was opened, I could appraise my knowledge and wisdom. Between the balancing of my feelings, thoughts, awareness, strength and wisdom, I could see the universe as it truly was.

I was exposed to a level of learning that was impressive. I felt that way because I came across information and theories that explained some of my own personal encounters. It was difficult oftentimes to explain or share some of the transpersonal exposures, especially with others who might not have had the same frame of reference, but it was extremely consoling and awe-inspiring to read a text or come across information that substantiated my experience.

I also learned firsthand that when I knelt down to pray, I could not offer only the ailing parts of me for healing. I had done that all my life and being specific on the portions I invited Spirit to touch was self-serving. It never worked. Offering my heart to Spirit began my soul's journey and brought healing into all aspects of my life. Whatever healing I was searching for took a new form, shape and attitude each time I surrendered.

Upon reflection, I see that the transition period of my life just prior to my injury was focused on all work and no play. I had become so serious that I lost the humor and fun things I loved to do. I had by then also lost more trust in humanity because I felt that others enjoyed pushing me down further, especially when they knew I could not fight back. As my dear friend Adjoa (*A-jo-a; for a girl born on Monday*) expressed eloquently, "We allowed a lot of people to dump their garbage in our backyards until we had no room to dump our own." With each dumping I allowed I lost personal power.

The same transition period brought me experience of the depth and compassion of the human heart because a lot of friends and family cooked, grocery shopped and offered many other things without my needing to ask. It was during those times and expressions of empathy that I knew the universe knew my name, Mensimah. I knew that it mattered to others that I was here.

I learned about my own misconceptions about healing, and from where they really came. I recognized the anger I expressed toward everything held me back from feeding my passions. My desire to fight was one of the reasons I stayed alive. My fears, especially in my dreams, were an illusion that separated me from inner truth. They fueled my desire to retreat. My sadness and depression pushed me towards change, and my joys, even in the darkest of times, expressed my desire to live. Then my perceptions shifted and the constellation of my experiences, qualities and values brought a joy of living a richer life for my Community and myself.

Tompala

Tompala, Tompala
The sound of the talking drum beats,
waiting to hear your voice.
Shio yomo, shio yomo
The swishing sound of the wind whispers
clearing the way to hear your song.
Zi gli gi
The hand of the clock unwavers,
A reminder it is time.
She cries Allah in a black gown asking the reason behind the
mindless death.
Nobody hears her, nobody reacts. Silence.
She shivers in a pale blue shapeless gown, forced to recount the
experience of being violated.
Nobody hears her, nobody reacts. Silence.
She's black and blue from a punch too many. We encourage her to
honor and obey her husband or lover.
We pretend, we hide.
She holds the frail child begging for milk, with flies swarming above
the head and moans of anguish.
We dig a grave spreading rich soil, thanking Spirit for the memories.
The earth is barren without your powerful steps and voice, woman.
Tompala, Shio yomo, Zi gli gi
The drum is talking
The wind is whispering
The clock unwavering
It is time.
Rise Woman!

Mensimah Shabazz 2004

CHAPTER 7
The New Journey

In the Akan tradition it is believed that our ancestors are responsible for the gift we bring to our life's journey. My journey began with ancestral presence developed through a shamanic journey. Shamanism is a form of religion practiced by indigenous peoples of this world. Often accompanied by a power animal or spirit guide and drumming, the shaman retrieves spiritual information through visualization and imagery in order to heal self, others and the community. The shaman also retrieves lost life-essence from the under, middle and upper worlds.

My interest and practice in shamanism occurred accidentally even though it seemed like I had been waiting for it all my life. I attended a seminar at the Institute of Transpersonal Psychology in California titled "Journeys of Transformation" which was led by Dr. Michael Hutton. I had the opportunity to fully engage in a variety of sessions on shamanic journeying, and African spirituality. And something spectacular happened.

During one of my journeys, I was standing on top of a hill with outstretched arms. Within my view was the ocean and Elmina Castle near my hometown of *Oguaa* (Cape Coast), on the Gulf coast of Ghana. The castle was the last stop before native people from Ghana were loaded onto slave ships. I heard wailing, moans and cries of anguish coming from the castle. In the background, there were drums and singing. My heart pulsated gently in my chest, as I was urged to welcome home some of the slaves' departed spirits.

I knew I was being called to serve. I accepted the call without hesitation and with that unsolicited vision I came to terms with my destiny. I have focused on the practices and rituals of shamanic divination since. My most recent teacher, Jeannette, brought honor to my pursuit of shamanic wisdom and continued to help me bring my experience and medicine to the world. A very gentle woman, Jeanette is a psychologist who has integrated shamanism into her practice with such tremendous success. She shared her knowledge, wisdom and counseled me with such calm, it resonated to the core of my being.

The importance of this particular journey cannot be over emphasized. It sealed my dedication to my spiritual path and allowed me to practice it with grace. With love, knowledge, wisdom and respect for the earth, I pour libation to my God in celebration of my spiritual journey, my bonding with my ancestors and the culmination of events that rekindled my interest in the traditional ways. I also noticed that some of the intuitive abilities had resurfaced during my illness and heightened as I continued my spiritual practice.

I have reconnected with a supreme being, *Nyankopon*, and the spirits and deities of my culture, including rivers and the wind. I worship in the ways of the indigenous people with the belief in one supreme God. I participate in the community while preserving my personal power. I strive for humility, but I am not servile.

If I could dance like I used to, I would jump to express my spirit to the heavens because for the first time in my life I understand that expression of spirit must endure all challenges, but cannot do so without new practices and teachings. The fact that I recognized a clear path to healing, my willingness to transform my relationships and unmask my anger and all its disguises, did not mean my work was done. In fact, it was just beginning.

There is an African proverb that says that "it is with the aid of the tree that a tree climber makes contact with the sky." I had positioned myself at the trunk of the tree, intending to make contact with Spirit. It was with the guidance of spiritual teachers that I was able to climb high enough to experience transformation and growth. With renewed interest, I pursued psychotherapy, astrological counseling and metaphysics.

I spent some time with Maureen who is a Master Herbalist and also my metaphysics teacher. She helped me reconcile some of the dreams I had which I had difficulty understanding and interpreting. A very slender and reserved woman, she shared her expertise in precise detail and our weekly meetings in her home office opened me to a world I did not know existed. I learned about Akashic records, other terms and concepts that deepened my search for a new reality. The process allowed me to open and accept multi-dimensional states of being.

My friend Sam referred me to Dottie, my psychotherapist. Something familiar happened the first time I saw her. I had the same feeling I had when I attended physical therapy with Shirley, except this time the feelings were deeper. I had this sense of peace and I just wanted to sit on the couch and sleep. Dottie had short, well-coiffed blond hair and she exuded confidence. She opened her conversations compassionately making it easy to trust her. I let my guard down without being coaxed. By our third session I opened myself totally, which enabled me to further process the deepest areas of my suffering. I talked about my rape for the very first time in almost 30 years. But there were a lot more unresolved emotional issues to talk about, so Minty and I went to Anguilla, in the Carribean, where Dottie lived and worked, to continue my healing.

On the first leg of the trip to Anguilla, there was a stop in San Juan, Puerto Rico. I sat on the plane hoping I could convince the stewardess to allow my daughter to move into the seat next to me instead of sitting in front of me. While I wondered why the travel agent insisted she could not find two spaces for us together, I caught the sight of a young boy at the corner of my eye sitting by the window all alone. When I turned to look at him, he was weeping so hard it was heartbreaking. It was painful to watch him cry, and I struggled to hold back my own tears.

I reached across the empty seat between us, holding out my

hand. He looked up at me and reached across the aisle, placing his little hand in my own. His tiny hand felt warm and moist from wiping his teary face. I also noticed a large card hanging around his neck, which indicated he traveled alone. I began to talk to him. "What is your name?" I asked. He responded quietly sobbing, "Rafael". "What is wrong?", I asked gently with concern. His response was incoherent. He spoke Spanish. I did not want to take the chance of having him repeat his explanation so I asked the gentleman in front if he could translate. The man turned sideways and asked him why he was crying. Through the help of this translator, Rafael expressed his sorrow in leaving his mother behind in the States while he traveled to spend his vacation with his father in Puerto Rico. Though I was unable to see the harm in visiting his father, I empathized. The questions made him cry some more. The depth of his sadness became my focus. For a few minutes, I moved into the seat next to him and just held him for a while without saying anything. As his tears subsided, I tried to reassure him that everything would work out just fine.

He seemed to quiet down and almost simultaneously, the stewardess gave me the go ahead to move my daughter into the middle seat. The three of us traveled together as a family until we arrived in Puerto Rico. Just before walking off the plane, I looked at him and he had the biggest smile on his face almost as if to tell me that we would both be okay. He probably could sense my own pain. If we were to believe in fate, it was obvious that this incident was not just a coincidence. There was a significant reason why I met this young boy that day.

In the flash of a second, my thoughts raced back in time

to when I was ten years old. I was on a bus traveling to boarding school and all the uncertainties and pain of that moment resurfaced. Unlike this young boy, I did not weep for what I had lost. I held it all in. His tears allowed me to bring forth the tears I never shed. It was a powerful healing moment for both of us, especially for me.

This trip to Anguilla was intended to spend time with my psychotherapist and for healing. The jolt I got to revisit the first most painful incident in my life was powerful. In fact, it was almost as if I was being nudged to really do my homework and do it well by starting from the beginning and my first trauma.

In Anguilla, my sessions with Dottie were intensive and we covered a lot of ground. She helped me recognize, claim and conquer my rage. But I believe I made headway in such a short time because of what she brought to the process. She did everything well. She integrated humor, could relate culturally and her love of life and for life was infectious.

The cumulative experiences resulted in another significant leap in my personal growth. I felt that I had become more comfortable with myself as a woman. Prior to this and probably all my life, I felt that everything associated with being a woman carried a lot of weight, responsibility and difficult choices. I did not feel at all liberated. I felt more burdened. The African culture, with a complex values system, traditions and social systems, places different standards and expectations on women. There was a form of indoctrination that taught a woman to be submissive especially in a relationship with a man. I resented that idea. I became detached from that process. Then I had the added baggage. The first time I experienced trauma in my life at *Mmofraturo*, women perpetrated seemingly devious acts and the preconceived notions I had about how honorable, gentle and nurturing women were went down the drain.

I also observed how women were treated in my culture and I did not want to do the same things when I grew up. On one hand women were honored in their traditional roles as care-takers and nurturers, as the bearers of knowledge and love. On the other hand, they virtually did everything else and suffered in silence. While some women carried loads on their heads to get from one place to another literally, it translated into their lives figuratively even if they lived in affluent homes. The manner in which women were treated was not limited to the uneducated or poor. And that was not encouraging for me. I separated myself emotionally from my femininity.

But this was a new time, and I was open to new wisdom associated with being a woman. I have felt the blooming of my breasts during my menses and appreciated it. Reliving this as an adult has enabled me to find a new level of sensuality by embracing my body. I have spent several weeks with a group of women in a circle, meditated, healed and shared experiences meaningful to our existence. I know now that I do not have to smother the woman in me in order to survive, nor do I have to shun the role to avoid the observations I made just before puberty. In fact, it is by accepting my femininity that I can bring awareness to issues like rape, physical and emotional abuse in communities such as mine and help reshape tradition.

I believe that women are born in the perfect image of the goddess and should be treated as such. That begins with understanding and knowing the true meaning of love, including self-love. Unfortunately, current understanding benefit men, and even our legal systems are not able to stop the torture, abuse and murder of women in the name of love. I remember so clearly after I was raped that I would have preferred to talk to a man. This was not because I trusted men more than women, but because I believed that a man would be less likely to blame me openly for what had happened. I believed that other women would react to me as someone who stirs up the community's emotions by bringing up issues that people want to pretend do not exist and would suggest that I must have done something to attract that attention.

The most crucial development would require women to support one another in solving problems such as child abuse, abandonment, incest and runaways. Women have the right to disagree with each other. But I believe that there are certain situations where we need to find common ground, because they affect our children.

I believe that men have been successful in keeping women apart because it is a male dominated world, but women have kept themselves apart by believing that they can gain power only by either siding with men or defying them. I believe that when women do not measure their power in relation to men, they use their nurturing spirit to make this world better.

What we don't need is a society where one gender controls the other. In a balanced society, the stimulating energy of men should complement the nurturing and healing elements within a woman. But more profound is the fact that we should be flexible in making decisions that may deviate from a moral code of an ideal woman, *obaa sima*. Losing oneself in another in order to find and feel love is a sacrifice of a woman's innate beauty and the love that the ancient mothers inspired.

The prescribed stages that lead a woman toward wholeness include being a daughter, a house-holder, and a mother. But even as a woman passes through those stages, they should not define her. "A woman is a nurturer, ritualist, teacher and wise woman." By surrendering to that kind of love, a woman is free to discover herself in any of these roles.

Becoming a mother has been one of the most intriguing experiences of my life. I have enjoyed being a mother to my beautiful child, and I feel intrinsically happy that she chose me as her mother. My daughter is the manifestation of the divine within. There are challenges in raising her, yet each joyful challenge presents an opportunity for renewal and a new beginning.

The first time I reached out to feel the cuddling from my ancient mother *Yemoja* for strength, was when I confronted the deep buried secret of my rape thirty something years ago. As I lay in her lap, I realized that I had yearned for that comfort all my life. How different my life could have been if any other woman in my community had shared her experience or truths to enable me understand that I had done nothing to cause the rape.

As a believer of truth, I hold the vision of the holy feminine within me now. I relate to the regal, beautiful, gentle, passionate and wise matriarch of this earth. I recognize the life force of women and believe that each one of us can find love, peace, joy and growth in our life experiences. We can touch each other through spiritual practice. I once dreamed that six other women and I, from different parts of the world, were summoned to follow different paths toward the same destination. When we gathered there, we followed an old wise woman into a room and stood in a circle. Within that circle was a tiled floor with a big gemstone of a different color where each woman stood. As we reached out to hold hands, each gem lit brightly and formed rays of every color imaginable. As the rays of color converged at the center of each stone, its top changed into a white spot and lit the sky.

This dream conveyed to me a powerful message of the value of every woman's unique gifts. We have our own stories and different paths to travel, yet we unite to affect personal, societal and spiritual changes that reclaim the goddess in each of us and on behalf of the world. It was also a dream about forgiveness. Forgiveness is not only a medium to heal yesterday's pain and sorrow; it opens the door to self-awareness and love. Through forgiveness, my mind and soul were freed from the shackles of the past. Forgiveness also enhanced my capacity to trust my life's work and have faith in the process. I am guided to ask for forgiveness from those I have hurt by my actions as I forgive those who had, in different ways, impeded my growth on this journey.

By asking for and offering forgiveness, I reclaimed my personal power and took responsibility for my thoughts, emotions and actions so that I am able to stand by them in spite of other's expectations. It is the process of knowing and honoring self, which ultimately sustains the comfort, joy and love in my life. I harness my personal power by defining the role I want to play on this earth.

During this current period of change, transition and growth, I decided to continue my studies and I have successfully completed my Master's degree in Transpersonal Studies, with a concentration in women's spiritual development at the Institute of Transpersonal Psychology in California. I am currently pursuing my doctorate in psychology. I found my studies of the transpersonal to be synchronistic because my exposure and understanding of being, altered states and meditation, validate my life experiences. More importantly, I have met some of the most compassionate people who share common wisdom and values.

Physically, I am able to walk with less pain than I used to. I still have a limp, sometimes with fluctuating and exacerbating pain. Even though I may not remember how it felt living without pain, I am more inclined to use these sensations in my body as a trigger to how balanced I am emotionally and spiritually, and that serves me well. The totality of my experiences helps me to transform and move into the future with confidence.

My life's work, as I see it now, is as an activist for social justice, especially for women and children. I must be free to speak my truth universally, without allegiance to any ideology, – for I believe personal truth resonates with everyone irrespective of social standing or affiliations. I envision a world where there is peace, where no one would find pleasure in acts that involve the intentional harm or killing of innocent beings. I envision a world where our individual and collective efforts yield respect and healing for the people and populations that have been molested.

I would know a world where the laughter of children will

touch hearts and vibrate directly to the heavens, as mine did when I was a child. And I would know a world where we would all be respectful of Spirit's design for our natural resources.

In facing my life's challenges, there were many opportunities to lay down my burdens by picking up the gems in my life's lessons and carrying them forward. In hindsight, if I weren't raped all those ancient years ago, I may not believe that sexuality and sensuality are very important aspects of who I am as a woman. If I had not been injured, I would not understand the impermanence of life and the importance of being present daily in my life, nor would I have yielded to my soul's yearnings to experience love, joy, peace and abundance.

I am who I am today because of all my life experiences. I embody those events, both happy and sad, and I could not have gained the knowledge, empathies, emotional maturity and wisdom if I had not gone through each one. There are no regrets on this journey of mine, and that is the true meaning of *Sankofa*! I have gone back to fetch what it is I left behind.

There is an African proverb that says that "If you have wheat, share it". I learned and embodied this proverb from the way Grandpa Sardis lived his life. I was blessed by his gentleness, and love for his family. He set very high standards for me to emulate. And I have begun to integrate my grandmother's energy and ancestral connections; where I grew up, the people I grew up with, and the influences that have shaped my views and spiritual beliefs as I dance into the future.

In an indigenous culture such as mine, where the media plays a minimal role in defining morality, our role models come from family and communities and our respect for ancient wisdoms. My grandmother embodied the sacred feminine – a woman who was graceful, gracious, and spent her time teaching and sharing thoughts and experiences to further the growth of other women. Having her in my life as my Spirit Guide has been a profound experience for me. I wept when I saw her, grateful for her presence. She encouraged me to face my fears about stepping into my power and doing my life's work. She is my gift!

I also define who I am by my mother's strength, courage, integrity and discipline. Heaven knows I needed discipline. Through her, I have learned the value of taking responsibility for my actions and moving through my life's challenges with determination. She shaped my character. I am who I am by my Aunt Araba's fearlessness as a woman. I learned to express my true feelings without intimidation. I am who I am as well, by my sister's generosity, by my brother's selflessness, and most especially, my daughter's energy, intuitiveness and compassion. She has graced my life with warmth and unconditional love. It is my hope that when she has a child, he or she will be as good to her as she has been to me.

I have been many things to different people, and the truth of who I am lies in my integrity. I come from a culture where being responsible, disciplined, and honorable to self and family is written into our moral code. It is easy, therefore, to develop and extend honor and respect to all individuals irrespective of social standing, race and creed. I have always stood for the things I believed in and have even been ostracized for it. That may have effectively silenced me for a time; it has not changed my beliefs.

Although I recognize that I prefer the different perspectives I gain from working behind the scenes, when necessary I step forward and speak or act in ways that support my beliefs. I moderate my power in many situations because of my love for people and my need to balance my feelings with my message. In essence, that is what makes me a warrior and a healer. It is my gift.

There have been times when I was not who I was supposed to be, but by Spirit's grace that is no longer so. I have a deep, strong, full and open heart. I used to think that was a weakness. And I admit that it made me more vulnerable when I did not set boundaries. However, today I am able to extend love effortlessly towards all. I am grateful for my life and for all those who share this life with me.

It is said that knowledge brings responsibility. My responsibility is to move toward wholeness. My spiritual and transpersonal experiences are not limited to my identity as an African woman. The universe is open to me, and I am empowered to live up to my highest ideals.

Beginning with my childhood ability as a seer, I have known that there is more than one vision of God. Traditional worship, personal freedom in thought and expression, my vision of a new and compassionate world and my dedication to justice for women and children guide me on my soul's journey. I know who I am. I am a medicine woman and this is my healing story!

I Am

I am a woman born in the image of the goddess
with infinite wisdom, beauty and grace.

I am a woman who has grown up and known
the depths of darkness

losing my virginity through brutality but yet it did not

taint or dwindle my feminine power.

I am a woman who was blessed in that moment and arose to

experience the energy that connects me to Gaia and Spirit.

I am a woman who knows that no amount
of torture, ridicule can change the natural flow
of energy that fertilizes my heart.

I am a woman fiercely loyal to causes that uphold
the dignity of all women.

And as a woman, I recognize the love, unity and friendship

that binds all women to the goddess.

I am a proud mother, aunt, daughter and sister

who relates to the vastness of a woman's love.

I am a special woman in a man's world,

born to be adored by my lover.

I yield my soul to the glory of Spirit

that I may proclaim in praise of the sacred that

I am above all else a goddess.

Mensimah Shabazz, 2002

Bibliography

Anderson, Sherry Ruth & Hopkins, Patricia. (1992). *The feminine face of God: The unfolding of the sacred in women.* New York: Bantam Books.

Angeles, Arrien. (1992). *The four-fold way: Walking the paths of the Warrior, teacher, healer, visionary.* San Francisco: HarperCollins.

Arewa, Carmen. (1998). *Opening to spirit: Contacting the healing power of the chakras and honoring African spirituality.* London: Thorsons.

Conway, D. (1988). *Magic: An occult primer.* GBR: Aquarian Press.

Dogo, Giuliano. (1981). *Guide to artistic Italy.* Milano: Gruppo Editoriale Electa.

Gagan, Jeannette. (1998). *Journeying: Where shamanism and psychology meet.* Santa Fe, NM: Rio Chama Publications.

Mares, Théun. (1995). *Return of the warriors: The toltec teachings – volume one.* Cape Town, S. Africa: Lionheart Publishing.

Maslow, Abraham H. (1968). *Toward a psychology of being.* New York: Van Nostrand Reinhold Company.

Millman, Dan. (1995). *The laws of spirit: Simple, powerful truths to make life work.* Tiburon, CA: H. J. Kramer, Inc.

Moore, Thomas. (1994). *Care of the soul.* New York: Harper Collins.

Peck, Scott M. (1978). *The road less traveled: A new psychology of love, traditional values and spiritual growth.* New York: Simon & Schuster.

Sams & Carson. (1988). Medicine cards: *The discovery of power through the ways of animals.* Santa Fe, NM: Bear & Company

Thich Nhat Hahn. (1998). *The Heart of the Bhudda's Teaching: Transforming suffering into peace, joy and liberation.* New York: Broadway